To really appreciate what Jesus did for us, we need to understand the difference between law and grace and how faith plays a pivotal part in this understanding.

# THE GRACE
## I NEVER KNEW

2018

Copyright © 2018
Tribute Publishing LLC
Frisco, Texas

Tribute Publishing, LLC

The Grace I Never Knew
First Edition September 2018

All Worldwide Rights Reserved
ISBN: 978-0-9998358-4-5

All Rights Reserved. No part of this book may be reproduced, stored in a retrieval system, or transmitted, in any form, or by any means, electronic, mechanical, recorded, photocopied, or otherwise, without the prior written permission of the copyright owner or the Author, except by a reviewer who may quote brief passages in a review.

Printed in the United States of America.

In God We Trust.

## CONTENTS

Forward ............................................................... iii

Introduction ......................................................... ix

Chapter 1 – Grace I Never Knew ........................... 1

Chapter 2 – Culture and Change ......................... 17

Chapter 3 – Are You Operating in Law or Grace? ...... 27

Chapter 4 – Experiencing Spiritual
                Blessings in Christ ..................... 41

Chapter 5 – What I Learned About Grace
                from My Pet Chickens ................ 63

About the Author ................................................ 73

The Grace I Never Knew

## FOREWORD

This book is a powerful reminder of how we sometimes get in our own way and how change starts in our own minds. Mathew Joseph shares that the way you believe and accept your gifts, in your mind, will drive your attitude and behavior.

I always tell people that we are born perfect in God's eyes, fully prepared to succeed, but along the way, we might not see whose we are and what we're capable of achieving through Him. Life happens to us and we start engaging in bad or unhealthy things. We might begin to abuse alcohol, drugs, food or something else. We might start getting angry, depressed, or create unhealthy addictions, thoughts or actions. Sometimes we completely redefine who we think we are, due to the confusion and deception in this world. However, God's message is very clear: If you have been saved, you have been saved by grace, through faith. You just need to believe in Him, accept Him and live who He created you to be.

When you were born, do you remember that tag made of flesh attached to your side? You know, the one that said, "addict," "depressed," "anger issues," "fearful," "worried," "confused" or something else that was negative?

No, you say? You don't remember having that or even being born with an extra flesh tag with a negative description of yourself? Of course not, because it wasn't there. The reason it wasn't there is because God never put it there! This is the part where you might say, but I do have a defining negative characteristic and it is a part of me, but I've always been that way! This is where I tell you that you are wrong. God never gave you any negative defining characteristics. That was all your doing.

Living in a world dominated by sin, causes us to sin. Sometimes, we can sin so much and for so long that we can get confused and accept the sin as our own identity. We can confuse what we DO, as who we are. I challenge you to accept and believe that the things you DO, really aren't who you are. I'm not talking about shirking responsibility for your actions, I am talking about separating what God made you to be, versus what you have added to your life through what you DO. If you are doing things you shouldn't be doing, stop doing them! Once you stop doing those things, you will remove from your life what you brought in or introduced. God never intended those things to be there in the first place.

Sometimes, we do negative and sinful things for so long that we can cover ourselves in those things, hiding who we truly are. When diamonds are mined from the earth, the seekers can be deceived as they sort through thick chunks of carbon. However, if they can keep their eyes on the prize, not on the nasty carbon, the seekers can and usually will find the brilliant gems inside, covered by the years of darkness. It can be difficult to sort through thick layers of dark decay.

Our lives with Christ are similar to mining diamonds. It requires great work to remove the layers of carbon to reveal the brilliance of the beautiful diamond inside.

Through grace, God has given us His brilliant, shining light to be found inside, just like a brilliant and precious diamond is found embedded with layers of black, hardened carbon. The challenge is that some of us have hidden the brilliant light within, by covering ourselves with layers of dark carbon, represented by years of sinful nature, negative actions, and habits. Some of us have been sinning for so long that we have falsely accepted the layers of carbon as a part of who we are. When we do this, we allow the layers of darkness to prevent God's brilliant light within us from shining to the rest of the world, assuming we have accepted His light: Jesus.

The great news is that although you may not feel like you can remove the years of negativity or darkness that you may be trapped in, God loves you and He can! He makes all things new! He can help you remove the years of negative and sinful things that have been hiding His light inside of you if you only know Him! Yes, you and God started your life journey and it will be just you and God who will end your life journey together, if you know Him.

Will you be prepared to give an account of what you did according to His plans for your life?

In this book, Mathew shares powerful insight to help you discover how God has already promised and made a way for you to have an abundant and happy life with Christ, through Grace, that you too can know.

You can do it .... right now. Here is how:
The Bible says that the only way to know God is through Jesus. In fact, Jesus said, "I am the way, the truth, and the life. No one can come to the Father except through me." John 14: 6. This means that by asking Jesus into your life, you can know God, be forgiven of your sins and have eternal life in Heaven.

In your own words

- Pray and repent of your sins
- Confess that you believe Jesus died for your sins on the cross.
- Acknowledge Jesus Christ as your Lord and Savior, and
- Ask Him into your heart.
- Tell Him you want to start new.

If you said this prayer on your own free will right now, then congratulations, you have been saved by grace, through faith. Now, you need to continue to do your part and live your life in a way that honors God, by getting into a Christian Church that teaches about Jesus and the Bible. A next big step is reading the genuine words written by Mathew Joseph in *The Grace I Never Knew*.

Now go forth and make your life exceptional!

Mike Rodriguez
Global Evangelist, International Speaker, Best Selling Author

The Grace I Never Knew

The Grace I Never Knew

## INTRODUCTION

### Something Unseen Doesn't Mean It Is Not Real!

You may be a person that does not believe in a God, higher being, or even a higher power. Or, you may be a Christian that does not fully understand/believe everything from the Bible because you have not seen God, experienced Him in a personal way, or even experienced His Grace. This book is about the grace of God that we can experience by accepting His only son, Jesus Christ, into our lives.

If you are not in agreement with me, let me see if we can agree on some common areas that we experience in our day to day life. To travel together, there must be some agreement. So here we go.

Truth is defined as something that is:

- For all people
- For all places
- For all time

Let's see what things are experienced by all people, in all places, and at all times. There are a few things that come to my mind: gravity, electricity, and radiation. There may be others as well that you may be able to come up with.

There is one thing that is true for all these. Can you guess what it is? If you said, "They are unseen," you are correct. These unseen things impact all people, all places, and at all times.

So, we must agree now that even though they cannot be seen, we can know that it is true because we can experience it in our day to day lives. Take gravity as an example. It is the same in India as it is in the United States and China. We know gravity exists because we are not floating. We are positioned on our feet because there is a downward pull to the center of the earth. Therefore, we can drive a car, walk, and run without being afraid that we will float off. Can you imagine what our experience on earth would be like if there was no gravity? We don't even think about floating off as an issue when we travel. Why? Because people like our teachers and our parents have taught us about this truth. We have also experienced it in our day-to-day lives. When you experience it, you will defend what you have experienced. It becomes like a testimony, which no one can dispute with you. It is your own personal experience.

If someone is doubtful about this, one can go up on top of a swimming pool diving board, jump into the water, and see which way you go, up or down. It is always going to be down when you are living here on earth. This is true for all people, all places, and at all times.

How about electricity? We cannot see the electrons, but when they are sent from a power plant through a metallic conductor, it channels electricity that is experienced by all people, all places, and at all times. Electrons are not seen. So, if someone doesn't believe that electrons exist, they can experience it when they touch the metal conductor that has electricity running through it. Believe me; I became a believer several times when I was a young lad when I touched the electrical conductor accidentally. I have even felt electricity at 220 volts. I will never forget that experience as electricity was felt by my whole body. Again, something unseen impacting our day to day lives. The more we experience this unseen thing called electrons, the more we can be confident and defend our experiences.

If someone from a remote part of the world tells you that he has not experienced electricity and tells you that there is no such thing as electricity and electrons, you know that he is speaking untruth because you have personally experienced it yourself. You have benefited from it yourself, and you have seen electricity impact many other people around you. In fact, your whole life revolves around the fact that there is electricity. It powers all of the appliances in your home. Electricity through the car battery helps your car to get started. We experience such distress and inconvenience when there is a power outage. Everything comes to a halt in our lives when there is no electricity in our home.

My friend, we can continue examining like this for all the unseen things that impact our lives every day. What I am saying is this: the things that hold this universe in place are unseen, such as gravity, electrons, radiation, etc. Even though you don't see them with your eyes, it doesn't mean they do not exist. Now I went through these examples so you can see that there is a God that is unseen and experienced by billions of people all over the world. They have experienced this uncommon God just like I experienced the uncommon God. Just because you don't see Him with your own eyes doesn't mean He does not exist.

When one starts experiencing the love and mercy of God, then it becomes a reality to the person experiencing it. In the Bible, David had this intimate experience with God when he was just a shepherd boy.

David the King realized and experienced God and wrote about it in Psalms 23. Even though he was now a King, he knew that it was God who took care of him and who brought him to the position of King. He admits that even though he is the king of Israel, he is still a sheep. Sheep are not considered to be smart animals. Sheep tend to wander off and get lost. He knew that in this life, he needed God, who proved himself strong when he was a shepherd boy. He experienced God's power and victories in his private life when God gave him the strength to kill the bear and the lion that came after his sheep. He knew from past experiences that God is a good God and God always took care of His people, just like a shepherd takes care of his sheep. God had given him private victories when he was all by himself in the field and he knew that God could help him now in public as the King of Israel. He knew that if God was his shepherd and he is the sheep, then all he needed to do was be in the presence of the Good Shepherd to get the managed care. Therefore, David said, "GOD, my shepherd! I don't need a thing. You have bedded me down in lush meadows, you find me quiet pools to drink from."

This is only available when you are in His presence. A sheep that wanders off from the shepherd and the fold is not under the managed care. But we have an uncommon shepherd in Jesus. He, the uncommon shepherd, said that if he had 100 sheep and one left and wandered off and left the fold, then he would leave the 99 others and go after the lost sheep, find it, and bring it back to the fold to give managed care. If the sheep wander for a long time, is lost, and cannot find the shepherd, the sheep is not under the managed care of the Shepherd. The wool covering grows long and heavy, it is not combed, things get lodged in it and can get caught in the bushes, and insects can make a home in the wool coat of the sheep. The sheep is not able to take care of its own, especially if it falls sick, because the Shepherd is not there. There is safety in the managed care of the Shepherd. The Shepherd knows that it is not safe for the sheep to be by itself. There are predators out there. Therefore, the sheep also need to be around other sheep.

Therefore, in the same way, you need to be part of a community of believers. God uses people today to bless you. The Holy Spirit may speak to an individual and say to them to go hire you for his company. The Holy Spirit, although not seen, is a great connector and comforter to us in our lives. The more you experience the unseen God and the Holy Spirit through fellowship with other like-minded people, the more you will come to know the goodness of God. Experiencing the goodness of God will make God a reality in your life. Even though you don't see Him, you will experience Him daily through reading of the Bible, fellowshipping with other believers, and experiencing the managed care of the Good Shepherd, Jesus Christ. You will not need a thing, you will lie down in lush meadows, you will find quiet pools to drink from, you will catch your breath, and He will send you in the right direction. Even if you go through deep, trying times in your life, you will not be afraid as He will walk by your side. He will prepare a great meal for you in front of your enemies, he will lift your head when you are tired and exhausted, and he will bless you abundantly!

Even though we do not see God physically, when we look around, we can see God in His creation and the world. Did you know that a point near the equator of the earth moves at 1000 miles per hour? Because of gravity, we move with the earth and do not notice the earth's daily rotation. Another amazing fact is that the earth revolves around a sun that is 93 million miles away from the earth. Everything is in such order for us to live. We can clearly see His handiwork in the creation of the world and mankind. In Psalms 19:1, it tells us that the heavens declare the glory of God and the sky is proclaiming His handiwork.

Also, our whole body is so complex, yet we do not even think about it on a day-to-day basis. It is fully operational and functioning on its own. Did you know that the human body makes the lubrication needed for our bone and cartilage and its joints to function properly? Additionally, the human heart is an amazing organ as it pumps approximately 1.5 gallons of blood every minute to supply food and oxygen to every part of the human body.

*(https://astrosociety.org/edu/publications/tnl/71/howfast.html)*

Since the creation of the world, His power is seen through his workmanship. (Romans 1:20). Even we are fearfully and wonderfully made by God (Psalms 139:14)

We are so busy with our lives that we don't even think about all these things. God takes care of all these things. We do not even have to worry about it. We are fearfully and wonderfully made. The whole world is kept in balance by our God. All we must do is put our full trust in God and believe in God, our creator. He knows how to take care of us. All we must do is be in His presence and be obedient to His plan and purposes in our lives. I hope I have at least made you think about an amazing God that loves us so much that He holds the earth and the universe in such balance where we do not even have to worry about these things. He also does not want us to just struggle with our lives. He has already made a way for us to live a balanced, fruitful life by accepting Jesus Christ, His son, into our lives. This book is about my lifelong understanding of this amazing Grace. I did not understand this marvelous Grace when I started my Christian walk and journey. As the years have gone by, I have come to understand a glimpse of the vastness of this Grace that is so freely given to us. I pray that this book will bless you and give you a better understanding of this marvelous Grace!

In this book, I want to highlight the following areas:

- Grace I never knew
- Culture and change
- Are you operating in law or grace?
- Experiencing spiritual blessings in Christ
- What I learned about grace from my pet chickens

The Grace I Never Knew

# CHAPTER 1

# Grace I Never Knew

I was born and brought up in a spiritual family in India. I came to the United States when I was nine years old. I gave my life to Christ when I was thirteen years old in New York City. I had a very good spiritual upbringing. I grew up seeing and witnessing "signs and wonders" and deliverances as seen in the book of Acts in the Bible. My dad had an amazing healing and deliverance ministry that helped me to understand and experience the healing and delivering power of God. In fact, I would be remiss if I didn't say it here, that my faith was strengthened through witnessing the supernatural. I understand many today have not seen or witnessed the supernatural like I have seen it. In fact, I used to testify about what I witnessed through my dad's ministry to others. I used to testify about my dad's amazing faith. However, I struggled with my own faith.

I grew up thinking that my acceptance with God had everything to do with my performance. My overall look in life was that I must do good to receive good and that if I did not meet the mark or do good, then I would receive the curse and judgment demanding of the unrighteous act. I used to always walk around in fear and doubt as I tied my faith in God with my own performance and wrong thinking. In fact, I used to believe that my salvation depended on my performance. I used to see God as a demanding God rather than a God who supplies and supplies it freely. I didn't understand the truth of salvation was by grace through faith.

## Chapter 1 – Grace I Never Knew

(Ephesians 2:8) I always did things to please my dad and mom more than making it a priority to please my God. And there is only one way to please God, and that is through faith. In fact, the word says, "without faith, it is impossible to please God." (Hebrews 11:6)

As I was growing up, I used to struggle with thoughts, bad thoughts. It used to make me feel bad and I would isolate myself from others. This was not healthy as I was always the "quiet" and "shy" one and did not have a community of friends growing up. For some reason, back when I was a teenager, our Indian culture gave more acceptance to such people than the ones that are outspoken and colorful. Because of this struggle, I never reached out to others and did not have any long-lasting friends. I never really had a community outside of our spiritual church community and even that was mainly only on Sundays and occasional church events. I used to spend a lot of time helping my dad in his ministry. I did this as a sense of duty rather than a "calling." I did finally, by the grace of God, get out of this thinking and saw my ministry to serve as a calling from God rather than a sense of duty.

As I matured in Christ and reflected on my life, I found out that this was a very dangerous place to be at: alone, isolated and without a real community of friends and confidants. I used to internalize everything and struggle with personal sins and habits. I really didn't feel comfortable talking about this with anybody, including my own parents. I thought that I would have to live like this until I died. I never saw the light at the end of the tunnel for this problem. As I matured in Christ, I learned that those thoughts were not my thoughts, but it was the devil's thoughts. I now resist those thoughts and bring them to captivity to the Word of God that is resident in my heart. (2 Corinthians 10:5; Psalm 119:11) I now know that I have the authority to use and access to the "armor of God," "word of God," and prayers in such times. (Ephesians 6:10-18)

I don't know what happened, but my thinking about my heavenly father and the grace of God was totally twisted and not in line with the Word of God. I saw and thought of the love of God and the grace of God as conditional and always demanding rather than unconditional and freely supplying. I used to think that God's acceptance of me was based on my performance, always! I would have to keep up with a set of standards and rules to continue to receive acceptance from a demanding God and my church community. These standards and rules came from the Old Testament, the church, the Indian culture, and myself. Some of the rules that I followed, erroneous as they were, mistaught me and I accepted it as truth. I always thought that the more I performed and met the demands of the law, culture, and standards from my parents and myself, then I would be acceptable to God and continue in God's love. I was never happy and became very self-absorbed and very self-conscious that I never could fulfill all the demands placed on my life. I couldn't do much for the Lord, and if I did, it was from a sense of duty. Most of the time, I was running on empty, so to speak, not experiencing the freedom in Christ. This was even tougher because my father and mother were in the ministry and we were held up to higher standards. The spiritual bar was set high as I was a preacher's kid. Don't get me wrong, because the bar and standards were set high for me, even though I did not meet it fully; I was in a better place than most of my counterparts. Many of my counterparts got into trouble and some, due to their reckless living, died prematurely. Because the bar was set high, life was very tough, and sometimes I feel like I missed out on my childhood in the areas of recreation and fun. Anyway, I don't have any regrets as God has me in a much better place now. I want to help as many people, including my own children, with the good news of the Gospel so they can lead a blessed and fulfilled life. I also want you to know this grace of God that is so rich and free and liberating!

I was in an identity crisis. Spiritually, my mind had taken on an identity as an orphan, or even sometimes as a foster child, rather than a natural son of God. I was always seeing my heavenly father as an angry, always demanding, and judging God. I viewed God as very hard to please due to the performance-based demands placed on my life. You see, the orphan or the foster child always has this mentality that he or she must be well-behaved, obedient, following rules all the time. If they don't do that, they have this dreaded fear that they will not be accepted and will have to go to another unfamiliar family. They move on in life with constant doubts and fears that they will not perform satisfactorily and at any time be moved to another family. They will always be very self-conscious and not move in the freedom that is found in sonship. The orphan must prove themselves before they are accepted into the family and given a status of the son or daughter. The orphan always goes around feeling as though they "do not belong" to the family. As the demands of the caring family grow, the orphan finds out that the acceptance is only based on his/her performance and that it is not "unconditional." They don't feel accepted and they feel like they don't belong. I found out later in life that this is what happens when you are operating under the old covenant of law. Law is very demanding and based on performance-based righteousness whereas grace is always supplying and based on rest. This grace can only be experienced when self-performance is replaced with the mindset of resting in grace.

## Chapter 1 – Grace I Never Knew

There are two births mentioned in the following Scriptures in Galatians. It shows the two ways of being in a relationship with God. One is from Mount Sinai, where the Ten Commandments, or the law, was given and depicts a slave life, producing slaves as offspring. This is the way of Hagar, the bondwoman. The other birth was from Sarah, a son that was born of the promise. A good explanation of what I was going through is better explained by Brother Paul in Galatians 4:21-23:

$^{21}$Tell me, you who are bent on being under the Law, do you not listen to [what] the Law [really says]? $^{22}$For it is written that Abraham had two sons, one by the slave woman [Hagar] and one by the free woman [Sarah]. $^{23}$But the child of the slave woman was born according to the flesh *and* had an ordinary birth, while the son of the free woman was born in fulfillment of the promise.

As you can see, just like Isaac, those who follow God are children of promise. I was not living like a child of promise. I was not walking and living free from the performance or law mentality. I didn't realize fully that I was the righteousness of God in Christ.

## This is what 2 Corinthians 5:21 tells us:

*"For he hath made Him to be sin for us, who knew no sin; that we might be made the righteousness of God in Him." (KJV)*

Every time I committed sin or when I had a bad thought, I thought I was the worst of sinners and that I was not going to be victorious in my faith walk. My walk was based on the Word of God, but it had a lot of ups and downs. I felt like I was in a roller coaster, sometimes I was making it and going higher and higher, then all of a sudden, I would be going downhill again, just like a roller coaster. I was questioning my faith and looking down on myself. I would sometimes fast and pray, hoping to get acceptance and favor from God. I would hear the same kind of testimonies from church members of how they were fighting with the devil the past week and that they became victorious by the end of the week. Some were struggling with sickness and would say that God gave them the sickness to keep them strong in the faith. I would hear testimonies from believers that magnified sin and satan rather than the magnifying Jesus and the power over sin in the name of Jesus!

As the years went by, I would take up the Bible and read and learn that I am no longer a slave to sin, but I am a child of God. (Galatians 4:7) I was the righteousness of God in Christ and that Jesus' work on the cross was a finished work. (John 19:28, 30) I realized that I have a choice: either walk and magnify and give voice to my sin and live as a slave to sin, or walk as His beloved, greatly loved by God and as a servant of righteousness. I had to accept the fact that there is now no condemnation for those who are in Christ Jesus. (Romans 8:1) I was being pulled back into trying to fulfill the Old Testament laws and performance-based requirements. I was also very much trying to please many in the church who were using the mixture of law and grace. The Word clearly says, "You cannot put new wine in old wineskins." (Matthew 9:17) I found out that I am under grace and no longer under the law. Grace supplies while the law demands. This is the gauge that I use to find out if I am operating under the law or under grace. I often check myself now to see if the situation or the decision that I am about to make is "demanding." If it is, then I know it is not of grace. For example, the feeling that I have to read my bible every day for at least 30 minutes and if I don't I am going to have a very bad day is an example of a "demanding" decision. All throughout the day, if

## Chapter 1 – Grace I Never Knew

something went wrong, I would think that it was because I didn't spend enough time with God. Anything I did, whether in word or deed, including my appearance, had to be perfect or holy, and that God or the people around me would not be pleased otherwise.

After understanding the gospel of grace, I found out that I am accepted in the beloved, even if some days I do not read the Word like I should or even if I miss church or am late to a church service. I also used to feel that I must participate or be there for all of the church programs every week. There was a time I was going to church four to five times a week to participate in all types of ministry to gain acceptance and church positions. Sometimes church leadership will demand things from you that will cause you to neglect your family and relationships. Grace tells me that my first ministry is at home. Thus I should not neglect my family to go after the ministry. I now know that God works things out to get me the acceptance and positions within the church to help further His kingdom work. There is ample supply from God who consistently supplies. When you go by the seashore, you see the waves that are continuous and never-ending. God's grace is like that; it is wave after wave of supply that is continuous, right on time, and plentiful from God. It is already there for us as we come into His presence and depend on Him for everything! In fact, in Philippians 4:19 the Scripture says:

*"But my **God shall supply** all your needs according to his riches in glory by Christ Jesus." (KJV)*

This identity crisis continued in my life for a long time. I was also condemning myself for personal struggles and failures. This crisis continued until I started to hear about the real depth of grace and the wideness of God's liberating truth.

## Chapter 1 – Grace I Never Knew

My faith started to grasp the depth and the width and the breadth of God's unconditional love towards me and this was demonstrated to me with the finished work of Jesus Christ. (Ephesians 3:17-19) I don't have to perform to gain acceptance anymore. I am accepted in His son Jesus Christ, His beloved! I found out that it is the "truth that you know" that sets you free to live a life of freedom from self, guilt, shame and condemnation. (John 8:32)

Taking on the wrong identity can paralyze you. It will keep you from achieving your God-ordained goals in life. One of the biggest dangers of this identity crisis is that someone else can steal your identity and try to make decisions for your life that can paralyze you or keep you from achieving your purpose and destiny. You want to be able to make your own decisions. David in the Bible overcame by not taking Saul's armor off. We see this in 1 Samuel 17:28-47.

As you can see from the Scriptures referenced above, there were **multiple people** that were messing with David's God-given identity. They were trying to frame him differently than the way God saw him. You must be careful that you walk in your God-given identity. God has a clear plan and purpose for your life. You need to pursue God and His ways and not what others tell you. You must hear the voice of God yourself. The only way you can get to know the Good Shepherd's voice is by being like David: be in His presence and have a relationship with Jesus, the true Shepherd. How do you know the voice you are hearing is true? The Word of God is your source for hearing God's voice. The bible says, "My sheep hear my voice," and "No strange voice will they listen to." (John 10:27, John 10:5) David knew God's voice because he used to spend a lot of time with Him as a shepherd in the field. He used to sing of God's creation and his experiences with God. In the field, he learned to hear and experience God personally. Trust the Shepherd of your soul, Jesus Christ, and you will not go wrong. You will reach your destination with joy and gladness. You will live an abundant and fruitful life. The problems, heartbreaks, loneliness, fear, doubt, and worries may come in your path, but knowing that there is a good and loving Shepherd taking care you will calm your heart and mind always. (Philippians 4:7) Guilt, shame, and condemnation will not affect you as you will walk in the God-given identity and as a child of the promise. (Romans 8:1) The more you experience Jesus' unconditional love for you, the more you will be appreciative, satisfied, and at rest with your life.

David was destined to be a king! He didn't know that at this time before his battle with Goliath, but God had set up conditions and situations to take David there. David knew who His God was because He had intimate fellowship with Him as a shepherd boy. God was always near to him. He had personal experiences with God when he was all alone in the field tending to his sheep.

Eliab, his brother, first belittles him by saying, *"What are you doing here! Why aren't you minding your own business,* **tending that scrawny flock of sheep**? *I know what you're up to.* **You've come down here to see the sights, hoping for a ringside seat at a bloody battle!***"*

Eliab came against his livelihood, or his occupation, saying that by just the job he does, he is not qualified to fight the giant, Goliath. He was saying to David, "you are scrawny because you tend to the scrawny flock of sheep!" Eliab tried to tag David's worth to his occupation! This is not the way God sees us; He always sees us with uncommon value, God-ordained purpose, and targeted destiny!

## Chapter 1 – Grace I Never Knew

We see next that David ignored his brother and looked for someone else that could help him understand why the heathen Goliath was mocking God Almighty, the God that he knew and had a personal relationship with in his private life.

Next, he turned to Saul, the King, and Saul belittled him and told him:

> *"$^{33}$ Saul answered David, "You can't go and fight this Philistine.* **You're too young and inexperienced**—*and he's been at this fighting business since before you were born."*

Saul looked at David's stature and compared it to Goliath! Saul was looking at the large stature of Goliath the giant and was scared. This was not the case with David! David was looking to his God, who is greater! How did David know his God was greater? He knew because of the personal and private victories that he had with God when he was all alone by himself in the field taking care of the sheep.

Keep in mind, David was very confident, not because of his own efforts, but because he knew of a powerful God who was with him in the field. He knew from his past experiences that God helped him to defeat the bear and the lion and delivered him from danger. Notice David's confidence was in the Lord! God supplied him with courage and strength to defeat the lion and the bear! Then David gives credit to God in verses 34 to 37. He had such great confidence in his Almighty God! Similarly, our confidence should only be in God. If you reflect on your life, you will be amazed at how God has taken care of you to the present. You will realize that He delivered you from a big car accident, a big fall, an incurable sickness, financial bankruptcy, depression, and natural disasters. You will see how good God is with your personal victories, just like David. When David was tending his sheep for his father, there was a time when a lion and bear attacked to devour the lamb from his flock. God had given him the courage to go after the lion and the bear to kill them and rescue the lamb. His detailed account showed that he would grab the predator's neck and wring it and kill it and that he would do the same to this giant who was making fun of God's troops. He was confident that the God who delivered him from the lion and the bear would surely deliver him from this crazy giant. David was very confident in his Lord! When we have personal victories in our lives, we will have a similar confidence to face all giants because we have experienced God in the past and seen how faithful He was in our lives.

Next, Saul tried to fit his armor on David. It paralyzed him and prevented him from moving freely. Similarly, we can knowingly or unknowingly become immobile or slow. My prayer is that you will have personal victories in your private life, just like David, so that when you are put in a challenging position in a public arena, you will have confidence in the Lord that you will overcome. Sometimes we ourselves put on these types of armor that limit us in our thinking. This is what happens when we try to take matters into our own hands and say that it is by our own efforts that we achieve our goals. David knew that he would be an utter failure with Saul's armor. He was immobile and was an easy target for Goliath. David said, *"I can't even move with all this stuff on me. I'm not used to this."* David wanted to trust God for this battle and not rely on human thinking and efforts. David was reflecting on his private victories that gave him strength and courage to come against Goliath, the enemy who was coming against God's people. David knew that if Goliath was coming against God's people, Goliath was coming against God himself. David knew his God intimately, so he knew that with God he was going to be a winner!

Next, we see what David did:

> *⁴⁰Then David **took his shepherd's staff, selected five smooth stones from the brook, and put them in the pocket of his shepherd's pack, and with his sling in his hand** approached Goliath."*

He took what he was familiar with, the things that he would use to ward off predators in the field: a shepherd's staff, five smooth stones, and sling. God has already given us gifting and talents for us to use. We do not need to try to become what someone else wants us to become. We should not copy or aspire to use someone else's armor to achieve our goals. Let's ask God to reveal all the gifts and talents that He has given to us to fulfill our destiny. David was used to and very comfortable with the staff, stones, and sling. This is what God wanted him to use. I am sure God took charge after David used the sling and shot the stone towards Goliath. God took and directed the stones to where it knocked the giant down to bring the giant to David's level.

David proclaimed this out loud and was then able to use the enemy's sword, Goliath's sword, and use it to kill him.

The battle belongs to the God. When we understand the Grace of God, we realize that surely the battle belongs to the Lord! We fully trust and put our confidence in God's work and not our own works. We will join God in the work that He is doing, rather than having God join us in the work that we are doing! When we join Him in His work, we are guaranteed victories, 100%. "If God be for us, who can be against us?" (Romans 8:31) No one! When we rely on God's grace, we will see the problems that the enemy has brought, that appeared like mountains, now come down to our level where we will be able to get the victory. This is the grace of God, where we do not rely on our own strength and works, but fully trust God to supply everything we need to get both the private and public victories in our lives.

You must know that the devil and others are trying to steal your identity of how righteous you are in Christ. You are chosen by God, unconditionally – this is the grace of God. It is not by our works that we have been brought into the family of God. It was the grace of God and His pleasure to choose us while we were yet sinners. (Romans 5:8) You are adopted into God's family. You are now God's precious sons and daughters in the family of God. You are heirs with God and joint-heirs with Christ Jesus. (Romans 8:17) You have a wonderful inheritance. When you are his son or daughter, you have privileges and authority within the family of God to overcome. You must know that you are forever loved by God and nothing can separate you from the Love of God. (Romans 8:38-39) You have the mind of Christ, a mind that is alert, laser-focused, and under self-control. The Word says there is now no condemnation for those who are in Christ. (Romans 8:1) This includes self-condemnation. If you are in Christ, you are a new creation; old things are gone, behold He makes all things new! (2 Corinthians 5:17) You are an overcomer, a well-oiled and maintained machine putting out good, useful products. You have an identity in Christ! You have His mind. You cannot go wrong!

Hearing about the faith of Christ and His finished work helped me get out of this identity crisis. Understanding who I am in Christ and that all my acceptance is based on His finished work helped me to accept myself more and commit myself fully to Christ.

## Chapter 1 – Grace I Never Knew

The new mindset helped me to have a better attitude towards life. I was able to look at myself and others with compassion and love. I started to see the unsaved as lost sheep without a shepherd. I saw people as unconditionally loved by God. I started to see the value in all people around me. I am now able to love and accept others because I accepted myself as Christ accepted me. I am so loved by God that He died for me. I am precious to Him. The depth of His love towards me is so amazing. As I read the Scriptures, I can clearly see the grace of God to His sons and daughters, as well as the sinners. I no longer look at myself as a sinner, but a saint. Paul, in most of the epistles in the New Testament, refers to the saved as "saints" and not as sinners. This is where it starts; we are no longer sinners, but saints! Our mindset must change in this area. We are saints and the more you take on this identity, the more your attitude will change in that direction. We need to confess all the things we are in Christ, for example: I am an overcomer, I am blessed, I am walking in favor, I am the head, I am healed, and I am unconditionally loved by God!

As I have shared here, the way you see yourself in Christ is very important in your spiritual walk with Christ. Don't let anyone steal your identity. Don't allow yourself to define who you are by anything other than what Christ and the Word of God tell you! Sometimes we let our feelings and emotions of the past, or even the present, reshape our identity outside of what the Bible defines us to be. The best way to check to see if you have a stolen identity is to check your attitude and lifestyle. Check it with the Word of God. As you examine the Scriptures, you will find out that in some areas you have the wrong mindset of who you are in Christ. In Hebrews 4: 12-13, we see that the word of God is powerful, sharp, cuts through everything, and lays us open to listening and obeying the Word of God. We should be obedient to the Word of God as we cannot get away from it. It will continue telling you and directing you to how God sees you in Christ.

I am now 54 years of age. I felt in my spirit that I need to document some of the things that I have learned to help my children as well as others along the way to see a good and loving God and to show how to live this Christian life in total freedom and rest.

## Chapter 1 – Grace I Never Knew

# CHAPTER 2

# Culture and Change

You and I live in a world that is going from bad to worse. So many things are happening around the world that make us wonder whether there is going to be a good future for our children. For a society to survive, there must be a set of standards. Laws and acceptable ethics. Standards are being thrown out and situational ethics are being pushed. Political correctness is stifling needed discourse and debates to effectively solve various cultural problems the society faces. Many children are raised without any accountability and responsibility. Parental rights are taken away, abortion is pushed as an easy way out for bad choices, media is out of control as they push their own agenda, and alternative lifestyle is even taught in elementary schools. All these elements affect our worldview and how we fit into the whole picture.

It is very important that we understand what is happening with our culture. We need to get back to basics. We should not allow our children to be socially engineered by the media, liberal schools and colleges, and the government. We see from the Bible that the world is going to go from bad to worse.

The Bible says that *"evil men and impostors will go from bad to worse, deceiving and being deceived" (2 Timothy 3:13).*

We should take responsibility for our own children and start teaching kids right from wrong starting from a very young age. The church needs to have programs that will keep the kids in church so that they can learn and grow in a safe and loving community of believers.

But we know one thing: that the wheat and the tares will have to grow together because if the tares are taken out, the wheat will also get hurt. See Matthew 13:24-30. My prayer is that our children will be hungry for the Word of God, just like hungering for physical food. This is important because the Word of God is the truth, is very powerful, is full of wisdom, and gives direction for their future. One thing is sure, Jesus said that He will return, and we need to bring up our children in the ways of the Lord. *Now is the time to work and labor for our next generation. We must be intentional in our mission to spend quality time with our children. We need to raise up a generation that will be accountable and responsible for their actions. The place to start is with the mind.*

How is the culture shaped around us, you may ask? Well, I believe that what one takes into the mind and accepts as true affects the attitude, lifestyle, and finally, the culture. The only way you can change your life and culture is through your mind. The secular media is very good at this. They will repeat the lies repeatedly until the listeners accept it as true. Media is a very powerful force to change the minds of people, especially the young minds. I have heard of "cradle to grave" liberal agendas that impact a generation. Many grow up to not believe in their creator and if they do believe in a God, it is so twisted that God is a good God and He will never allow anyone to go to hell. We need to have a mind like the mind-of-Christ.

Philippians 2:5 says, *"Let this mind be in you that was also in Christ Jesus."* Jesus's mind was laser-focused, full of love and grace, and having uncommon self-control. The mind is a place

## Chapter 2 – Culture and Change

where it starts. It ends up making decisions for you. Your mind decides what you are feeling. Isaiah 26:3 says, *"Thou will keep him in perfect peace, whose mind is stayed on thee."*

Your mind and the way you think will affect your attitude. For example, I keep thinking that I am not going to amount to much because all throughout my younger years people have looked down on me and spoke negative things over my life. I keep replaying those words in my mind and I take it as fact after replaying it over and over in my mind. This affects my attitude in taking on new things and new opportunities. I don't take any risks as a result and miss out on opportunities that could have made my life easier and better. This negative introspection and acceptance of my past keeps me in the rut of passiveness and self-denial. I will compare this to a parked car. To move a parked car, it must be at least put in neutral where an outside force can help move the car out of the garage. In the same way, if we need others to help us with our issues that hold us back, we need to at least change our thinking.

In Proverbs 16:3, the word says, "Commit thy works unto the Lord, and thy thoughts shall be established." You can start accepting the Word of God into your heart and mind and start expecting and experiencing a wonderful and hopeful future. The way you do this is by what the Scripture says in Romans 12, verses 1 and 2. I have highlighted here the words within the scriptures having to do with the mind: **"transformed by the renewing of your mind; thinking; fix your attention; recognize; respond."**

Your mind is a place of your will, emotions, memories, thoughts or imaginations, intellect and feelings. It is a stockroom of gathered information. The areas of your mind help you to judge (I am guilty of this), store, remember, voice (yes, I have learned the hard way with this one), and create. This is where you take on your identity. Your mind affects your attitude, the way you live, and the type of culture you create around you, whether it is in your personal life, home life, or your corporate life. On a day to day basis, we fight battles in our minds. Some old, bad memories or feelings may pop up in your mind as you wake up one morning that will affect your attitude for the day. Sometimes we allow these emotions to run wild without controlling it. It leads to physical stresses, illness, and changes in our bodily functions. The Bible verse says, *"As he **thinks** in his heart, so is he" (Proverbs 23:7)*. This is also why the word of God in Romans 12:2 says, to:

> *"....be not conformed to this world: but be ye **transformed by the renewing of your mind**, that ye may prove what is that good, and acceptable, and perfect, will of God."*

## Body, Soul, and Spirit (What happens when you are born again and fully trust Christ for your Salvation)

If you are a Christian, this is what happens when we are born again and trust Christ for Salvation. You see, you are a tri-partite being consisting of body, soul, and spirit. (1 Thessalonians 5:23)

It is with your spirit that you worship and contact God. Your soul, which includes the conscious and subconscious, the realm of emotions, memories, thoughts and the will, gives you your personality, self-awareness, rationality, and natural feeling. Finally, your body is a complex physical creation by which you relate to this world and to other people in the world.

## Chapter 2 – Culture and Change

Your soul is not saved, thus need to be renewed daily by the washing of the Word of God. Your body is your physical body. This is where your senses are active like seeing, hearing, and touching.

Here, I want to address the area that is called the soul. How can we take care of it? The Bible verses in Romans 12: 1-2 tells us to do the following:

You must embrace what God is doing for you. Don't become adjusted to your present culture, because God wants to change it for the better. God wants to change your way of thinking by having you fix your thoughts and attention on God. This is how transformation will take place from the inside out. When you realize what God wants from you, you will intentionally and quickly respond to it knowing that God has the best for you. Don't be like some of your friends and family that are so accustomed to the everyday culture of spiraling downward to immaturity. Allow God to develop you into a well-informed mature person. Allow yourself to sit and listen to mature Christians who have gone before you and get Godly advice from them and pass on the Godly advice that you have received from God and fellow believers to your kids and grandkids. This will allow you to keep what I call the 'chain of grace' linking one generation to another.

God wants us and our next generations to change and go from glory to glory, from faith to faith, and from strength to strength.

- **Glory to Glory** means from glory of the law to the glory of the new covenant of grace. Paul speaks of the spiritual glory seen with the new covenant believer's spiritual eyes. A glory that will transform us into the image of God's beloved son Jesus Christ. (2 Cor. 3:11,18)

- **Faith to Faith** means from the faith of the Old Testament (based on our works and performance) to the faith of the New Testament (based on faith in Jesus Christ and performance) (Romans 1:17)
- **Strength to Strength** means going from one victory to another victory with various life experiences that may be good or even challenging. (Psalms 84:7)

Change is inevitable, and it is a choice on how we should handle change. The only way to change your life and culture is through your mind. Are we going to have the right attitude towards change? As we go through this life, we will have to change our thinking, attitudes, lifestyles, and culture. This can only be done by submitting ourselves to the Word of God. The change will need to take place in relationships, character, traditions, hearing, leadership, spirituality.

Change is always necessary to go from glory to glory, faith to faith, and from strength to strength. You can and should change yourself first. We change as we meditate upon the word of God and believe on the right things as it says in Joshua 1:8, "this book of the law shall not depart out of thy mouth, but thou shalt meditate therein day and night." As we meditate on the Word of God and believe that the Word is for our own well-being, change starts to occur through repeating and playing the Word of God in our mind. We start believing what the Word says; we are not basing it on our feelings, emotions, or memories. You cannot force others to change. Conflict arises when you try to force your views, thinking, experiences, and conduct on others.

## Chapter 2 – Culture and Change

Jesus clearly gives us some sound instruction in Matthew 7, verses 1 to 5, to not pick on people, jump on their failures, and criticize them for their faults. If you do, you are bound to be treated the same way by others. The more we get into the Word of God and understand His unconditional love and the forgiveness that we have through the richness of His grace, the more we are able to understand that the love of God is so extravagant, unconditional, and the opposite of human thinking that we must be able to also love and forgive others. Jesus even instructs us to love our enemies, which can only be done by the power of His Holy Spirit. God wants us to change from the inside out. God wants to see a true change in our heart, a circumcision of the heart. God is the one who will bring about the change in us and shows us a better way. The result is that He will lead us into greener pastures and will make us lie down and rest. We just must be in His presence and yield our will to His will. God does not want us to have a critical spirit and look down on others with a holier-than-thou attitude. I believe God wants us to look for the good in others. God wants us to think and meditate upon things that are lovely, pure, and of good report. (Philippians 4:8) I also believe the more we understand God's grace of unconditional love, forgiveness and acceptance of us, we will be able to supernaturally love others, even the most unlovable. When you are moving towards change, seek God & His righteousness. You will not go wrong. Change is messy. It can cause relationships to be distant. Change of mind with a focus and direction is best. What you play in your mind affects your health. In 3 John 2, it says, "Beloved, I wish above all things that thou mayest prosper and be in health as your soul prospereth."

The mind of Christ will help us to change our attitudes towards our self and others around us. We will not see others in a negative light. We will always see them as a child of God. We will see them with a compassionate mind and heart.

Mahatma Gandhi, an Indian activist who led the Indian independence movement against British rule, employed nonviolent civil disobedience that led India to independence and inspired movements for civil rights and freedom across the world. Mahatma was able to change the mind in people that led to a cultural change in India.

In his autobiography, Mahatma Gandhi wrote that he read the Bible seriously and considered converting to Christianity. He believed that in the teachings of Jesus he could find the solution to the caste system that was dividing the people of India. Unfortunately, when he entered a church, the usher refused to seat him and told him that he should go worship with his own people. The mindset and culture of the church was not amicable for Mahatma Gandhi to worship there. I am hoping that Mahatma, eventually, gave his life to Christ, before he died. I love this quote from Mahatma!

"Your beliefs become your thoughts,
Your thoughts become your words,
Your words become your actions,
Your actions become your habits,
Your habits become your values,
Your values become your destiny."

— **Mahatma Gandhi**

The Word of God, in 1 Corinthians 2:9-16, has promised to us believers that "we already have the mind of Christ!" This is awesome! God has planned and purposed great things for us, His beloved children. (Ephesians 2:10) We receive the

## Chapter 2 – Culture and Change

Holy Spirit when we give our lives to Christ and come under His provision and care. (Acts 1:8) He reveals the things of God to our inner spirit through the Holy Spirit and the Word of God. The secrets of God are revealed to us. He is our friend. Every day, the Holy Spirit will be dropping things of God into our inner spirit. When we read the Word of God, the Word of God confirms what the inner spirit has already received from God. Sometimes the Word of God will confirm what the Holy Spirit wants us to know for that moment. God's Word is wisdom and when we act according to the wisdom of God, the answers for the situation that we are facing will be divinely given to us. He has also given us the mind of Christ when we become His child. This mind is laser-focused, sharp, and very discerning. We will be able to discern what is right and what is wrong. The Holy Spirit in us will help us to discern the things of the Spirit and help us only to hear and listen to the voice of the loving God.

How do you react to the culture around you? Do you react or are you pro-active in preparing for the correct changes to happen in your life? One of the best ways that I deal with these changes is by playing it out in my mind ahead of time. I ask myself, "What if my spouse don't validate me the way I want to be validated?" or "What if my boss does not give me a good raise or bonus?" or how about, "How should I react when I feel like no one is there to help me?" Even then, I am to be kind and love them.

The Holy Spirit is there also to help us change for the better. The Holy Spirit was given to us when Jesus was resurrected. The Holy Spirit is our comforter, guide and our change agent. In Luke 6:32-36, we are instructed by Jesus regarding our response to life situations: He wants us to ask ourselves what we want people to do for us, and then become proactive and do the same for them. We are also told to love

## Chapter 2 – Culture and Change

not just the household of faith, but also the sinners. We need to give help without expecting anything in return. We are promised that when we do this, we will not regret it. We are instructed to love and live our lives like Jesus loved and lived. We are to be generous and kind towards others like Jesus.

We should not go with our thoughts, feelings or emotions. We should accept the Word of God and say that "I have the mind of Christ!" and that I will accept what the Word tells me to do and be obedient to the Word because the Word of God is the same yesterday, today and forever. I can change the direction of my thoughts with the Word of God. When this happens, my feelings and emotions towards the situation change. The best way to do this is by standing on the promises of God for that situation and claiming it for yourself. This can feel funny at times because what you are claiming and speaking out loud is different than what your thoughts are for that situation. I have experienced this. I can rely on the Word of God which can cut through the thoughts and even intentions of my heart. This is how change starts: in the mind first, then the words, then the actions, then the habits, then the values, then it affects our destiny and culture. By accepting the Word of God, and not giving in to our feelings and emotions, we will start and continue operating in Grace! The culture around us will not affect us as we have a set standard that we live by and that is the Word of God. The Word of God is unchanging. It is alive and will bring about the changes in our lives that will help us to accept and love all who come into our lives; to name a few, these include: spouse, children, friends (past and present), church family, and yes, even in-laws!

# CHAPTER 3

# Are You Operating in Law or Grace?

To really appreciate what Jesus did for us, we need to understand the difference between law and grace and how faith plays a pivotal part in this understanding. I struggled with this most of my life. I was so confused about this topic that I was questioning my salvation. I did not know any better. I thought that since Paul had problems in his own life in Romans 7:8-25, this was going to be my way of life also. I was reading this passage without understanding the difference between law and grace.

In summary, I was living my life on a performance-based mindset. As a pastor's kid, I was reading my bible, praying, preaching, teaching, witnessing, and helping with most of the church activities on a routine basis. I thought that the more I did this, the more I would be loved by my Heavenly Father and Jesus. I was putting requirements and expectations on myself based on what I heard from others and what I thought I needed to do. I used to get frustrated when I fell into temptation and couldn't measure up to expectations. I was on a legalism train in which I was the lead engine, so to speak. I had a holier-than-thou attitude and was pushing this on others around me. I was judging others based on my own achievements and spiritual level. On some occasions, I was very harsh to young believers. I was relying and pushing on my own self-effort rather than relying on the grace and enablement of the Holy Spirit. I would add or even take away

## Chapter 3 – Are You Operating in Law or Grace?

a metric or a measurement on what I thought goodness or self-control or even meekness looked like. Sometimes my performance metric was based on a political view that I strongly held. I still remember a time when I told one of my friends who was a Muslim that they need to look at this evangelist that I held up in high esteem that was so holy and pure in his actions. Within a short period, I found out the evangelist that I had put on a pedestal fell from grace.

Paul reminds us that we cannot please God based on our performance standards. We should base our righteousness on the performance of Jesus Christ and His completed work because God bases our righteousness on Christ; we are considered saints! (Ephesians 2:19; 1 Corinthians 14:33) In fact, Jesus said, "It is finished!" (John 19:30) His work is a completed work, and we are reminded that there are no vacancies in the Trinity. We should not step in and try to take the place of the Trinity in any respect. We should accept the fact that God the Father, God the Son, and God the Holy Spirit are perfectly happy with Christ's performance on earth as well as on the cross and now in heaven! We should also realize the following: God saves sinners by grace alone, through faith alone, in Christ alone.

I grew up thinking that even Paul had the struggles that I am facing. I have heard so many preachers and messages that highlighted these verses and conclude that even Paul, the one who wrote many of the epistles in the New Testament, had problems! This kind of thinking would give believers the wrong mindset and keep them from living in victory. When they go through struggles, they would fall back and say, 'Even Paul had struggled with sin and a defeated life.' I thought, 'This is the way it is going to be the rest of my life.' I started listening to preachers and teachers that understood

## Chapter 3 – Are You Operating in Law or Grace?

and showed grace unconditionally. I saw how they reacted and responded to the unreached, unlovable, unchurched, and the wayward youths. I saw with my own eyes how the Grace of God reached out to them and witnessed changed lives. I found out where sin abounds, Grace much more abounds! (Romans 5:20) I witnessed that the people who experienced the love and Grace of Jesus were serving the Lord and winning souls within a few months of their conversion. I allowed the Holy Spirit to do a work in me that was unbelievable. The Holy Spirit showed me that I had a strong religious spirit. I fell under conviction and realized that I had to change and only Jesus and the Holy Spirit's power could change me. I yielded my will to the will of the Holy Spirit. I am not the same person I used to be. In the past, I was very passionate about winning souls for Christ, but I was going about it the wrong way. I was not showing a lot of grace. In some cases, I was very judgmental, especially when others did not measure up to the holiness standard that I set for myself and others. I also used to self-condemn myself a lot of times when I failed to meet my own holiness standard. I was also emphasizing works I did to feel comfortable that God loves me. I felt the more work I did for the church and others, the more God would love me.

We don't have to live this way. We know that we are under the new covenant of God's Grace and no longer under the law. So many Christians do not realize the benefits of the new covenant and life in God's kingdom. In God's kingdom, everything is made new and we are very valuable to Him. Old things are gone and new has come in this Kingdom. (2 Corinthians 5:17) He wants us to be happy in His kingdom. To realize and fully benefit from life in this kingdom, we must have a revelation of this Kingdom and what He has accomplished to make us part of this amazing and eternal

## Chapter 3 – Are You Operating in Law or Grace?

Kingdom. Psalms 103: 1-5, says, "Bless the Lord, O my soul, and forget not all His benefits." All these benefits are purchased for you with His blood. **Knowing** our position in Christ and that we are made righteous only by Jesus Christ gives us many privileges in this Kingdom. We are given access and authority in this Kingdom. In this Kingdom, we know that we are totally forgiven by Jesus Christ. It is the **truth that you know** that will set you free.

We are justified only by Jesus Christ, not by our self-effort or works. Many Christians are clueless about this and thus live a defeated life and do not enjoy the good gifts and benefits that are already there for them in this Kingdom. The reasons for this lack of understanding can be many, including not reading the Word of God, not attending church, and not having fellowship with the saints. Jesus said, "Your faith has made thee whole." (Mark 5:34) If we don't see ourselves in this light, we will be prone to falling back on self-effort and follow the law and not grace, as Paul talks about in Romans. John chapter 1 verse 17 reminds us that the law was given through Moses and grace and truth came through Jesus. Instead of waiting on and resting in Jesus, we sometimes put forth a lot of self-effort and get frustrated. We will not live an abundant life this way. Faith cometh by hearing and hearing by the word of God. (Romans 10:17) The way we can overcome this lack of knowledge and lack of faith is by hearing, hearing, and again, hearing the Word of God.

But sometimes, we forget and start hearing the wrong voices. Jesus said, "my sheep hear my voice." (John 10:27-30) Where can we hear the right voice? We hear His voice in the praise and worship songs, in the Sunday school lesson, in the preaching, through your friends and families that are in the household of faith. Sometimes you can be in church and hear

## Chapter 3 – Are You Operating in Law or Grace?

the wrong voice because you are not learned in the Word of God. Therefore, one should be a student of the Word of God. Sometimes, you may be in a church that does not teach the true Word of God, a church that does not believe salvation is by grace through faith, does not preach Christ Crucified, or does not preach about hell." (Ephesians 2:8-9 & 1 Corinthians 1:23) This is where the Holy Spirit will guide you into all Truth. Ask, seek and knock for the understanding of His Kingdom. (Matthew 7:7-8) Rely on the Holy Spirit. He will never fail you. (Deuteronomy 31:6) In my case, even though I was in the church, I was not taking the time to learn the Word of God. Thus, when a preacher came and preached, I would accept what I heard as true gospel. I later found out that the preachers were pushing law and not grace. In other words, they were going back to the law and self-effort that Paul refers to in Romans 7.

The sad part was that the more I was listening to these types of preaching and not understanding the teachings on law and grace, the more I was living a defeated life. You see, what Paul was talking about here <u>was his life under the law</u> and <u>not under Grace</u>! Romans 8 highlights his life under Grace! This is very important to understand here. I went through most of my life thinking this was Grace living! My mind had taken on an identity that I will continuously struggle with sin all my life and I would be tripping up and falling continuously. This kept me from growing in spiritual life. I had a life of roller coaster Christianity. I was not understanding the Scriptures. I was taking it out of context and it brought confusion and wrong thinking which affected my attitude and the life I lived.

Per Paul, the Old Testament law, even though it was an excellent piece of work, sin found a way to pervert the

## Chapter 3 – Are You Operating in Law or Grace?

command into a temptation, making it a forbidden fruit. The law was no longer guiding him, but it was seducing him. Finally, he fell for it, and the law that was supposed to give him life was tripping him up and throwing him down headlong. Sin simply did what sin is so famous for doing: using the good as a cover to tempt me to do what would finally destroy me. Sin was making him more conscious of his sin. He was trying to do everything in his own effort. Paul was struggling to live a holy life, but wherever he went, sin was there to trip him up, and he would fall headlong deep into it even more. There was no way out.

He ends chapter 7 by asking a concerned question: "Is there no one who can do anything for me?" We go through the same kind of questioning in our lives. Many times, we are like Paul trying to do things our way and not settling in for the ways of the Lord. We put forth our best self-effort, only to find out that we were heading in the wrong direction. Sometimes we follow the wrong map for our lives and end up in the wrong place. We get frustrated and get upset with others and ourselves. We needed someone to get us out of this rut. *Jesus took care of this for us.* We did not have to do anything other than put our full trust in the finished work of Jesus Christ. This is what Paul is exhorting to us, that Jesus is the answer to all of our life's issues and problems. He has provided the correct map for us to follow. We don't have to get lost or end up in the wrong place anymore. We are given the right map to get to our eternal home. This map is Jesus Christ. He is our GPS and the destination is set by Jesus Christ for our eternal heavenly home! Our starting point should be set here on earth by believing on the Lord Jesus Christ! It was Jesus who set things right in this life of confusion and chaos. Jesus is the way, the truth and the life!

## Chapter 3 – Are You Operating in Law or Grace?

**Then Paul goes on to answer the question of who can help, in Romans Chapter 8. Paul says the solution is life on God's terms. The grace of God, in Christ, broke through and got us the victory from a lifetime of brutal tyranny at the hands of sin and death. We are no longer under the grip of the law but under the grip of Grace! Saving us was God's idea and this fateful dilemma was once in for all resolved!**

- Saving us is His idea
- We trust Him and let Him do it
- It is God's gift from start to finish
- We are in His Kingdom
- We don't play a major role
- This keeps us from bragging about it
- We don't make or save ourselves
- God does the making and the saving
- He creates each of us by Christ Jesus
- He wants us to join Him in the work he does
- He has shown us the good work that we need to do for Him
- We should be doing this good work.

There is a story of a small, malnourished orphan boy who used to attend a village school. The children brought their lunches and jackets to school and were instructed to leave them at the entrance of the school. On one day, one child's lunch was missing. When the teacher asked in anger, "Who took the lunch?" the small orphan boy raised his feeble hands. The teacher told the boy to come forward to receive the punishment. As he came forward with a guilty face, he stood there alone, weeping and trembling with his head down in shame. As the teacher was ready to punish this orphan boy, another strong boy came forward in a hurry and said, "I will stand and take the whipping in his place!" In front of the whole class, the strong boy positioned himself and received the punishment for the guilty orphan boy and paid the penalty for the violation of the rule set by the teacher in the school. What caused this strong boy to come forward to help this malnourished orphan boy? I would submit and say that it was his compassion and understanding of the orphan's plea that caused him to step out and take the suffering and punishment of the malnourished, forgotten, and hungry orphan boy.

A much greater love and grace was shown by our heavenly father when He sent His only Son to take the punishment of you and me and all the people of this world. Taking the other persons' punishment is another way of showing grace. Grace is defined as an unmerited or unearned favor. We do not deserve a pardon for our disobedience to God. But God showed us His unconditional love by sending His Son to die in our place. In His agape love, He sent His Son to pay the penalty for our sins and justified us to God. Justification simply means, "Just as if I have not sinned!" When we put our full trust in Christ and accept Him into our hearts, God looks at us through the blood of Jesus Christ. When He does this, we are white as snow! We have complete access to God through His Son Jesus Christ."

Thank God, saving us was God's idea and the result of all His work. All we do is put our faith and trust in Him to create each of us in Christ. It is His gift to us. Our success in life will depend on how we receive this gift. Do we receive it

## Chapter 3 – Are You Operating in Law or Grace?

freely or do we feel like we still need to add our works to it, to obtain God's acceptance?

Speaking of gifts, I want to share an example. Say, if you received a $1,000.00 check as a gift on your birthday. What do you have to do to benefit from this gift? Let's go through the steps:

- First, you will have to receive the gift. If you don't receive it, it is useless.
- You must take it to the bank and deposit the check. Then you wait to see if the check has cleared the bank. After it clears the bank, now you have the money in the bank for you to use it to buy goods and services.
- You still must either draw the money from the bank or write checks towards your account to withdraw the money. It is only then that you are benefitting from the gift that you received. This is the same case with the Gift of God's Son, Jesus Christ.

You must make it personal and **accept Jesus as your gift**, given to you by our Almighty God. God showed Amazing Grace by giving us His Son to bless us with every spiritual blessing in Christ Jesus. God is completely satisfied by what His son, Jesus Christ, accomplished on the cross. John 19:28-30 Jesus testifies to this:

*"Jesus, seeing that everything had been completed so that the Scripture record might also be complete, then said, "I'm thirsty." A jug of sour wine was standing by. Someone put a sponge soaked with the wine on a javelin and lifted it to his mouth. After he took the wine, Jesus said,*

## Chapter 3 – Are You Operating in Law or Grace?

*"**It's done ... complete**." Bowing his head, he offered up his spirit." (MSG)*

Jesus said, "It is done… complete." This means there is nothing else that God needs to do for the penalty of the sins the people commit. Jesus was the gift that God sent to this world to redeem us from the penalty of sin, which is death. When we receive Jesus as our gift, we are recipients of God's grace and we can start living a life of meaning and purpose. The more we receive Jesus as a Gift, the more we will understand the richness of this grace shown to us. We can start living the exceedingly, abundantly, above-all-that-we-can-ask-or-think life here on earth.

We are a new creation, created for His kingdom and placed in His Kingdom; He provides protection and provision and sets the rules for His kingdom. He wants us to join Him in the work He does. He does not want us to create anything new. He works in us the good works and we get so full of His goodness that it overflows into His kingdom to be a blessing to others.

I cannot depend on myself and my works, my obedience, my goodness and service. I must fully depend on God and make sure that I abide in Him, knowing that He will take care of me.

But when you depend on God's grace – His unmerited, unearned, undeserved favor toward you – that is when His promises become sure in your life. God wants us to totally depend on His grace, which is not based on our merit, positions and accomplishments. It is totally based on His favor to us. The Word says it is grace through faith that we are saved, lest we should boast. (Ephesians 2:8-9) When we

## Chapter 3 – Are You Operating in Law or Grace?

see Jesus in this light, we will fully start experiencing the promises He has given in His word.

To really appreciate what Jesus did for you and me, we need to go back to Adam and Eve's, Abraham's, and Moses' time. God had given Adam and Eve a choice as seen in Genesis 2:5-9, 16-17; 3:6.

From the beginning God wanted Adam and Eve to partake of the Tree of Life. However, the devil tempted them and convinced them to eat of the Tree-of-the-knowledge-of-Good-and-Evil. What the knowledge-of-good-and-evil does is makes us very self-conscious and performance driven. God did not want this for Adam and Eve. You may ask why, then, He gave them a choice. It is because when God created man, He made us with free will to decide whether to follow good and evil and to make choices ourselves. He did not want to create robots that follow every order from God. He gave us free will to make decisions on a day-to-day basis. Unfortunately, Adam and Eve failed at the first test. They did not choose the Tree-of-Life.

God had made the Garden of Eden very beautiful with all sorts of animals and plants and vibrant life. The devil tempted Adam and Eve by telling them that they can be like God and they fell and lost out on abundant living in a personal relationship with God. The tree of life must have had a role to play in maintaining the life of Adam and Eve. God wanted to be their source for all things. God wanted them to partake of the tree of life. I believe partaking of this tree would have given them abundant living without toil or effort on their part. God was to be their all-sufficient God. God wanted Adam and Eve to be dependent on Him for everything. He had great plans for them. Because of their fall,

## Chapter 3 – Are You Operating in Law or Grace?

God expelled them from the Garden and sent them to work and till the ground. Now they would have to work to live. Before, God was their source of life.

The covenant made with Abraham was grace based on God's promises. God told Abraham that he will make him a great nation, bless him, make him famous, a blessing to those who bless him and a curse to those who curse him. He also told him that all the families of the earth will be blessed through him. (Genesis 12:2-3)

During the exodus of the Israelites from Egypt to Mount Sinai, God dealt with the Israelites with grace. They complained a lot, and yet God showed them grace. (Exodus 14-16)

Fast forward to the time of Moses at Mount Sinai, we see that the Israelites all responded together, "We will do everything the LORD has said." To me, this sounds like self-confidence and self-reliance rather trusting God for His grace. I really believe in my heart that because of rebellion and arrogance, God gave Moses the 10 Commandments for the Israelites to follow, knowing fully well that they would not be able to keep them. I believe God really wanted Israel to continue trusting in Him for His grace and faithfulness. But the people said they would do everything God would tell them to do. They were trusting more in themselves rather than God's grace. I believe the Israelites were choosing the path of the Tree-of-the-knowledge-of-Good-and-Evil rather than experiencing the grace and faithfulness from the Tree of Life.

God knew this was the only way to bring the rebellious people to the end of themselves and at the end, to seek after

## Chapter 3 – Are You Operating in Law or Grace?

God, their creator, rather than the law and tree-of-the-knowledge-of-good-and-evil. I believe God's desire was not to give the law, but for the Israelites to trust and put their faith in Him 100%. As we read the Old Testament, we can see how things started to go from bad to worse as people tried to follow the righteous law. The law itself was holy, but the people could not keep up with the law. The law was very demanding. In fact, if one violated one of the Ten Commandments, then you violated the whole law. The law was very stringent and did not allow for any mistakes. The punishment was very harsh if one violated the law.

All the Old Testament stories leading up to the birth of Jesus Christ show the desperate attempts of people and culture trying to keep up with God's law and failing miserably. As time went on, Israelites and the priests brought in rules and regulations and commandments of men, which made living under the law very demanding, miserable, and hopeless. This era, from the time the Ten Commandments were given by God and up to the time Christ came (Tree-of-Life), was called the Dispensation of the Law. Law always demanded perfection, which the people of God could not achieve under the Law.

Therefore, Jesus told the religious people surrounding Him to "love the Lord thy God with all your heart, soul, and spirit, and your neighbor as yourself." (Luke 10:27) The only way to fulfill this command is to get back and experience the "Tree-of-Life" that God wanted from the onset, to put our full faith and trust in God's only begotten Son, Jesus Christ. Jesus said, "I have come to give life, and life more abundantly!" (John 10:10)

## Chapter 3 – Are You Operating in Law or Grace?

Jesus Christ is the only one through which we can experience the life God intended for His creation. Through Jesus Christ, we can get this abundant life back, where we are not seeking after knowledge of good and evil, but rather trusting God fully to lead and guide us into the blessed life that can be only experienced when you partake of the "Tree-of-Life!"

In His great love and mercy, God sent His only son to redeem fallen mankind. We see this in Romans 5:15-17

When we put our faith and trust in Christ for our salvation and eternal life, the promise is there in the Bible that we will be resurrected to see the Tree-Of-Life again in the middle of the Holy City with twelve kinds of fruit, a ripe fruit every month (Revelation 22:2-5). The leaves of the tree will be for the healing of the nations. There will no longer be any night or curse, and the access to the Tree-Of-Life will be reinstated in the New Jerusalem.

# Chapter 4

# Experiencing Spiritual Blessings in Christ

Paul is known as the apostle of Grace. He understood how God rescued him from his destructive path into the path of Jesus's marvelous Grace. He reminds us of how blessed we are in Christ and to allow for the eyes of our heart to be enlightened to know the hope of our calling and the glorious inheritance that we have in Christ. Grace is so free for the taking and receiving. Many times, we ourselves get in the way of this grace and don't receive it fully like Christ would like for us to receive it. It's all about the finished work of Christ's work on the cross. Along with what Paul tells us about this marvelous grace and spiritual blessings, I want to share with you how the Lord has blessed me and my family in America in healing, education, finances, and employment.

Paul's letter to the Ephesians is amazing because it informs us, through the Grace of God, how we become **a Christian**, shows us **how God wants us to live** the Christian life, and finally tells us about our wealth, inheritance, and walk in Christ. Paul wrote this letter from prison after his spiritual eyes were opened to see the **hope** of his calling, the **riches** of his glorious inheritance, and the incomparably great **power** at our disposal! We should be open to God enlightening our spiritual eyes to see, and understand what Paul is gently reminding us regarding our identity and standing in Christ! (Ephesians 1: 18-19)

## Chapter 4 – Experiencing Spiritual Blessings in Christ

Paul addresses his letter to the "saints" at Ephesus. Sometimes, we may not feel like saints. Life gets the best of us; we feel inadequate, beat down, and unworthy. The reality is that we are called saints, not sinners. This is because, when God sees us, He sees us in Christ and Jesus' blood cleanses us from all our sins and makes us holy and acceptable in the sight of God! Paul thus establishes upfront in his letter the "saints" identity in Christ. Paul also conveys that we have been **chosen** in Christ before the foundation of the world, we have been **predestined** into the adoption of children, we have been **accepted** in the beloved, we have been **redeemed** and all our sins have been **forgiven**, we have been **initiated** into the divine mystery, we have obtained an inheritance, and we have been **sealed** with the Holy Spirit of promise.

"Praise be to the God and Father of our Lord Jesus Christ, who has blessed us in the heavenly realms with **every** spiritual blessing in Christ." (Eph 1:3)

God is the reason, the source, and the provider of what we need to receive and keep the spiritual blessings. Paul knew the secret of tapping into the spiritual blessings in Christ was to have an account in "Christ's Bank." God is the source and depositor of the heavenly blessings in this bank. He blesses us according to His riches in glory!

Paul admonishes us, as saints, to access this supernatural spiritual bank account through prayer! When we are in the habit of prayer, we can consistently draw from Christ's Bank, by the power and help of the Holy Spirit. The Holy Spirit will comfort us, give us revelation, knowledge, and even bring people, places, and things we should thank God for and intercede for. When we pray, the Holy Spirit will guide

## Chapter 4 – Experiencing Spiritual Blessings in Christ

us and help us to really see, really hear, and really understand the hope of our calling, the riches of our inheritance, and the great power that is at our disposal! We need to pray such prayers that will make a difference in the world. God is working through those prayers!

There are two things that Paul teaches us about prayer. Firstly, how to pray, and secondly, how to pray the kind of prayers that have eternal impact and what we need to do to develop a deeper relationship with Jesus Christ.

**"I <u>keep asking</u> that the God of our Lord Jesus Christ, the glorious Father, may <u>give you the Spirit of wisdom and</u> <u>revelation</u>, so that you may <u>know him</u>." Eph. 1:17**

Paul gives us three words of advice regarding prayers: Keep asking, have a clear picture of who you are praying to, and you must know what you are praying for.

Paul also gives us 3 ways to focus our prayers:

- **See and understand the hope of His calling on your life**. When we understand the hope of **His** calling (not our calling) on our lives, we will realize that it is not about us. We will be single-minded, focused and have an attitude that says, "Come what may, because I know the One who has called me is faithful to help me complete it!"
- **See the riches of God's inheritance**. Romans 8:17 says, "Now if we are children, then we are heirs - heirs of God and co-heirs with Christ, if indeed we share in his sufferings in order that we may also share in his glory."
- **Tap into the power available to us as God's children and saints.** How can we "see" the power that God

Chapter 4 – Experiencing Spiritual Blessings in Christ

wants to make available to us? It is by and through the power of the Holy Spirit and the Word of God!

## Here's one of Paul's powerful prayers!

For this reason, I kneel before the Father, from whom his whole family in heaven and on earth derives its name. I pray that out of his glorious riches he may strengthen you with power through his Spirit in your inner being, so that Christ may dwell in your hearts through faith. And I pray that you, **being rooted and established in love, may have power, together with all the saints, to grasp how wide and long and high and deep is the love of Christ, and to know this love that surpasses knowledge-that you may be filled to the measure of all the fullness of God.** Now to him who is able to do **immeasurably more than all we ask or imagine, according to his power that is at work within us, to him be glory in the church and in Christ Jesus throughout all generations**, forever and ever! Amen. **(Ephesians 3:14-21)**

**In the Old Testament book of Isaiah 41:8-13 are also listed more blessings of God's goodness to us!**

We see here that God has done the following:

- Chose first
- Pulled you
- Called you
- Picked you
- Is with you
- Not dropped you
- Given you strength

## Chapter 4 – Experiencing Spiritual Blessings in Christ

- Helped you
- Held you
- Has a firm grip on you
- Is not letting go
- Is right here to help you

We should start seeing ourselves as God sees us and not the way we see us. We should start seeing ourselves in Jesus Christ only. We are His beloved! We are royalty! We are the head! We are overcomers! We are blessed! We are seated in the heavenlies with Christ! We are sanctified! We are Justified! Amen. Regarding our families, a husband should see his wife as a fruitful vine. The husband shall praise her! A wife should view her husband with respect. We should see our children as olive shoots around the table. (Psalms 128 and Proverbs 31.)

God spoke things into existence. He has given us the same authority to speak things into existence. There is life in the power of our tongues. Use your tongues to speak life into your family and situations. We speak and walk faith. We do not look at our problems, but to God who can solve all our problems. Trust Christ in all areas of your lives and He will take care of you! Stand on and speak out all the promises of God for you. Walk on the Word of God! Speak the promises of God in the Word over your lives. You will start experiencing God's grace in a powerful way! You will no longer see giants of the land, but a land filled with milk and honey (Exodus 3:17).

*"I handed you a land for which you did not work, towns you did not build. And here you are now living in them and eating from vineyards and olive groves you did not plant." Joshua 24:13*

## Chapter 4 – Experiencing Spiritual Blessings in Christ

I have experienced God's Grace, blessings and favor many times in my life. I would like to share some of the stories to bless you and encourage you to stay the course and experience God's Grace in the same way that I received it in my life.

When we put our faith in Christ and become part of God's kingdom, we experience God's consistent Grace. He works behind the scenes and goes ahead of us to prepare the way and bless us with favor with both God and man. God is faithful to do the same from one generation to another. Growing up, I was always taught, "Seek first the kingdom of God and everything shall be added unto you." (Matthew 6:33) This is what we believed in as a family and continue to do so. My parents also taught me the Bible Scripture from Psalms 23, "The Lord is my Shepherd, I shall not want; He makes me lie down in green pastures." He is like a good shepherd that goes ahead of the sheep and prepares the land for them to lie down and rest. We are the sheep and God is our Good Shepherd! In other words, God takes care of the hard work and toil from our everyday lives by opening doors that we would have never dreamed of or even planned. I want to share with you several events that took place in my life the last 43 years here in the United States. I am sharing these stories to build up your faith in God and to let you know that He is faithful to do the same for you in your life. He will go before you and work behind the scenes for your good just like He did for me. Buckle up; we are going on a faith-filled journey. My prayer is that your faith will rise within you and you will start experiencing this faith and continue to do so in the ever-increasing measure in your life!

My story will not connect without some personal history and background. Our family came to the United States in 1973

## Chapter 4 – Experiencing Spiritual Blessings in Christ

when I was nine years old. Writing this, I am now 53 years of age. My parents immigrated from India to the United States with only eight dollars. Back then, an immigrant family could only bring a total of $8.00. You may ask, why only $8.00? I could never figure this one out. This was the requirement back then and maybe it was to make sure a sponsor took full responsibility of us. Sometimes it is hard to figure out why certain laws and requirement exist. We just follow the laws to make sure we don't violate them and get into trouble with the immigration authorities. We had a family from New York City that God miraculously convinced to sponsor our entire family of five. Here's the event that led the family from New York to sponsor us to come to the United States.

My dad was a production manager of Caprihans, India PVT, LTD in Bombay, (now called Mumbai) India. He was a chemistry graduate. With his God-given talents and gifting, he ended up in management ranks. He was very successful in what he did. Along with his secular job, he was also very active in the Lord's work. My dad and mom had a heart of compassion and would go all-out to help people who were emotionally hurting and physically sick. Many people would come from all over India to our apartment for their healing and deliverance. After coming home from a long workday, people needing prayer for healing were gathered at our house. My dad had to shift gears very quickly and had to minister to the people. On one such occasion, a person was there for special prayer as she was getting ready to travel to the United States to be with her son and family. During the time of prayer, there was a prophecy through my dad regarding her daughter-in-law. He was foreseeing a serious and critical health condition and encouraged her not to worry, that complete healing has been promised by God. The

## Chapter 4 – Experiencing Spiritual Blessings in Christ

prophecy and the results came true. When the family went through this ordeal, they did not worry and experienced the peace of God. She got delivered out of the life-threatening problem very quickly. The prophecy was very accurate and because of their personal experience, the family from New York City sponsored our family to come to the United States in 1973. The reason for their sponsorship was this: The United States could benefit from and needed people like my dad who walked in the prophetic ministry to bless others. I am pretty sure that God, through the Holy Spirit and like a Good Shepherd, went before us and moved in their hearts to sponsor our family. This was the first instance where I saw God working behind the scenes for our family and going before us and directing our paths to favor and blessings. This is how we came to the United States of America and started our lives in New York City!

Yes, this is incredible! God used someone that we hardly knew and someone not even from our family to sponsor us to come to the United States of America! My dad was just helping and praying for God's people. When you minister to God's people, God moves on your behalf!

We moved to and lived in New York City from 1973 to 1978. My father worked as a New York Life Insurance agent, which took him to many cities in the United States. During his travels, he would continue to minister to people like he did in India. As he traveled, he saw many people having their own homes. My father's dream was for us to live in our own home. As he researched about home ownership, he found out that house prices were very high in New York City, while housing was very affordable in Houston. With a lot of prayer and guidance from God, we moved to Houston. My parents enrolled me in High School for Engineering Professions

## Chapter 4 – Experiencing Spiritual Blessings in Christ

where I made good grades and graduated 3$^{rd}$ (top 1%) out of around 600 students. This was great, however, my Standardized Aptitude Test (SAT) score was not that good. I scored 990 out of 1600. I was very concerned about my future and whether I would ever end up in a very good University. God had a plan and it was amazing to see it unfold as the days passed. He wanted us to experience His Grace and was going ahead of us and paving the way!

This is what happened on one day, known as Engineering Day at our school, when I was a senior in high school. Every year the university recruiters from all over the country would come and meet with the graduating seniors at our high school. There were many prestigious universities represented at our school from all over the country. I had made up my mind and was planning to apply only to universities within the state of Texas, such as the University of Houston, Rice University, and Texas A&M University. I was very close to my dad and mom and in no way was I thinking about attending a university outside of Texas. As I made my way from one college recruiter's table to another, I came across a table representing Washington University in St. Louis, MO. The recruiter behind the table was very nice and shared all the good things about Washington University and the reasons why I should consider them. I informed him about my low SAT scores to which he responded, "Don't worry about it. It is low, but your GPA is great so go ahead and apply." I was very surprised by his answer. I can now say, it was God who convinced the recruiter to consider me. He took my name and he told me to apply.

I applied to the University of Houston, Rice University, Texas A&M, and Washington University. Rice University put me on a waiting list only to find out later that I was not accepted. I was accepted to the University of Houston and Texas A&M and they offered me only student loans in the form of financial aid. However, this was not the case with Washington University; they not only accepted me, but also gave me a full ride scholarship for four years that was later extended for another year towards my Master's Degree in Mechanical Engineering. I am still in awe that I was accepted into this prestigious university with low SAT Scores. If I recollect correctly, a high percentage of incoming freshman students scored a perfect SAT score of 1600. My SAT score was only 990. This was an answer to our prayers to God. In this case, the Lord, through His Grace, brought the recruiters to my high school to encourage me to apply at their school.

During that time at age 17, I got my physical exam done and the doctor detected an irregular heartbeat. Upon further evaluation, I was diagnosed with a heart condition called Mitral Valve Prolapse (MVP). We were told that MVP is a condition in which the mitral valve does not close smoothly, causing abnormal heartbeats that may eventually become life-threatening. This was a very big concern to my parents as I was planning to attend Washington University in St. Louis. They sent me with lots of prayers and support. God's Grace sustained me throughout my stay at the university and I was able to finish my higher education within five years and graduated with a Master's Degree in Mechanical Engineering. God was so faithful in also healing me of this condition a few years later after graduation.

This is how I got my healing. One day during my personal devotion, I just put my hands on my chest and I told the Lord, I believe that you have already healed me. You are Jehovah Rapha! I receive the healing, in Jesus name! One day, as I normally was accustomed to doing, upon checking

## Chapter 4 – Experiencing Spiritual Blessings in Christ

my pulse on my wrist for an irregular pulse, I noticed no irregularity! To my amazement, my pulse was normal and beating regularly. Excited, I called my wife Soffee and told her all about my healing! She was also amazed, and just to be sure, we decided to go have a complete heart checkup. Praise God, the result from the heart doctor was that I had a perfectly normal and healthy heart! God's Grace provides us with healing. I knew later from reading the Word of God that the healing was already mine and God had already worked behind the scenes over 2,000 years ago through His Son Jesus Christ to get me the healing and victory! It was already a done deal; I had to just receive it by faith! Since then, I have received many healings in my own personal life.

I want to now share with you how I was able to start my home inspection and consulting business. I started my career with AT&T in Naperville, Illinois in 1986 after I married Soffee. Starting a business of my own was not even in my career plans. I tried to move up within AT&T with my own efforts and ran into several roadblocks. I felt like I was not in the network of folks that were tagged for management and promotions. They always looked at me as a technical type and not management type. Year after year I did my best to exceed the expectations placed on me by my management team. But God had other plans for me! After about three years, my ex-boss, who had moved to Mesquite, Texas on a company transfer, offered me a job with AT&T Power Systems, also in Mesquite, Texas. He also offered me the Tier 3 relocation package that was usually given to only high-level executives within the company. Later, I found out that I was their second choice and the reason I got the job was that the first-choice candidate's wife did not want to move to Mesquite, Texas from California. I saw this as the Lord going ahead of me and working behind the scenes to get me closer

## Chapter 4 – Experiencing Spiritual Blessings in Christ

to my family and loved ones.

In 1994, there was an opportunity to obtain the P.E. license in Texas without testing. This is unheard of in the professional engineering industry! Again, I experienced God's Grace and saw the Lord working behind the scenes to move an organization such as the Texas Board of Professional Engineers to waive the testing for obtaining the P.E. license. This was an incredible opportunity that opened for me. It was as if the Lord knew what I was going through. He knew that I was not able to move up within AT&T and that he needed to intervene to show me another way to bless me. The P.E. licensing would allow me to provide consulting services in the engineering field and allow me to start up my own engineering and consulting services company.

All this happened when I was working for AT&T Power Systems in Mesquite, Texas. I was not even thinking about becoming a professional engineer, let alone starting up my own business. This, I believe, was another life-changing opportunity and path the Lord opened and offered on a plate to me. I only had to fill out an official application form and submit five professional engineer's recommendations. I had to locate five professional engineers that I had interfaced with during my work with AT&T. I was able to locate them and requested of them to fill out the confidential recommendation forms and submit to the Texas Board of Professional Engineers (TBPE). I got all my material together and the Lord put professional and caring people in my path to help me get all the materials turned in to the TBPE.

I did receive my P.E. license and was asking God what I should do next. One day as I was reading the P.E. Magazine

## Chapter 4 – Experiencing Spiritual Blessings in Christ

in the bathroom, a small advertisement caught my attention. This ad said, "Have you ever thought about starting your own business?" I knew I was a recipient of God's Grace again! My spirit inside leaped with joy and I knew this was from God. I talked it over with Soffee and decided to pursue this opportunity. I was given real-time classroom and field training for a week by a professional engineer from Denver, Colorado. He was an unbelievable individual who I believe was sent by God to move me to the next level of my career. He offered the training to me for a very reasonable amount and certified me as a Professional Engineer Home Inspector of America, an organization that he started, to help other professional engineers all over America.

I was amazed at the timing of all the events taking place in my life. The Lord opened the door for me to start up an Engineering Home Inspection and Consulting Services business in 1994. The company name is RSH Engineering, Inc. I was doing this on a part-time basis while I was working full-time for another company. When I ended up making more money working part-time for my own company than the full-time job, I knew it was a sign from God for me to make the next move to leave and go full-time with RSH Engineering, Inc.

This was God's plan. He knew that He had to move me from Naperville, Illinois to Mesquite, Texas in order to become a professional engineer, start my own engineering business, and experience God's Grace, this time in financial blessings! I thank God for helping me to run and manage a successful business, RSH Engineering, Inc., to this day. I am also praying that I will be able to pass this business on to my next generation.

## Chapter 4 – Experiencing Spiritual Blessings in Christ

Now, I would like to share with you some stories regarding our family life. As I mentioned earlier, I got married in 1986 to Soffee and had four children. Our daughters are Rebekah, Sarah, and Hannah. Ten years after Hannah was born, God blessed us with Samuel, our only boy. Every man needs a son! Samuel was an answer to our prayers. God went ahead and paved the way for all three of my daughters' regarding their college education, especially in financial blessings. It has been said that God blesses the generations of his righteous ones that follow Him.

Rebekah, my first born, always wanted to be a doctor. She is not a quitter. She will strive to achieve her goals in life. To achieve her goals, she applied to the University of Texas at Dallas for the pre-med program in Neuroscience. She was a smart kid and achieved a very good standing in her graduating class. She got accepted to the college, however, we were not sure how we would pay for her education outside of taking student loans. She applied for what is known as a McDermott Scholarship, a prestigious scholarship. After waiting for a while, she found out that she did not get the coveted scholarship. She also found out that someone who was lower in the academic ranking ended up getting selected. She was sad. It was during this time that I had just completed my Executive MBA program at UTD, the same school Rebekah was applying for the pre-med program. As I was praying to the Lord regarding her situation, the Lord inspired me in my inner spirit and gave me the boldness to call the UTD's financial aid office to discuss why Rebekah was not chosen and what other options she had for her financial aid. To my surprise, the lady at the financial aid office was also concerned about why Rebekah did not receive the McDermott Scholarship. She then suggested to me that she was going to submit Rebekah's

## Chapter 4 – Experiencing Spiritual Blessings in Christ

name for the Terry Foundation Scholarship. She comforted me, saying that she will recommend Rebekah. A few weeks later, we found out that Rebekah was chosen for this prestigious scholarship. God and His Grace was now showing Himself strong on our behalf by continuing to bless me as well as my next generation.

After Rebekah finished her undergraduate degree at UTD in Neuroscience, she took the Medical College Admissions Test (MCAT). This is a test that is very important to get into medical school. She did not do well on the MCAT test, so she continued to pursue her Master's Degree in Health Administration so she would not lose any time in academics. She would try again for several times to get a better MCAT score. We even enrolled her in the Princeton Review program to help her to improve her MCAT Score.

It was during this time that my company, RSH Engineering, Inc., was not doing well at all. As I was praying regarding my business, the Lord led me to a Craigslist ad for an adjunct professor job opening at Mountain View Community College in Dallas. I, along with another engineer, developed two courses for two semesters that year: Introduction to Engineering and Robotics. The classes were successful, and the Robotics class included lab work. One day, I got the class going on their lab work and was sitting on a couch next to a coffee table. I noticed several blue books that were the same. They stood out, so I reached for one and started reading. It was a book that highlighted all the colleges that offered Doctor of Podiatry Programs in the United States. I noticed the requirements for admission, and to my surprise, Rebekah would have easily met the requirements for admission and was well qualified for entry into this program. I brought this book home and told Rebekah to consider the Doctor of

## Chapter 4 – Experiencing Spiritual Blessings in Christ

Podiatry program offered at Temple University as she was already in love with a person from the Philadelphia, Pennsylvania area. She did not take it seriously for a long time and I would remind her that there was a reason for my company not doing well for a season. The real estate industry was not doing well. My home inspection business thus was affected since fewer people were buying homes. I believe that God takes us from one place to other for a purpose, and in this case, it was to lead me to this blue book. God's Grace will guide not only our footsteps and paths but also our children's and our grandchildren's.

She continued to take the MCAT and would apply again to medical schools without any success. I reminded Rebekah again to apply at Temple University. One day, she agreed with me, applied to, and was accepted to Temple University. Another beautiful thing happened: she was in friendship with a pastor's kid from Philadelphia and they ended up getting married! Benjamin, my son-in-law, knew back then that one of my requirements was for him to have a Master's Degree. He strategically enrolled in graduate school and got his Master's Degree in Computer Science to improve the chances of marrying Rebekah. How wonderful is that? God knew ahead of time that she would marry someone from Philadelphia. Rebekah ended up going to Temple University in Philadelphia for her Doctorate degree! Today, she has received her Doctor of Podiatric Medicine degree and now is doing her residency in Allentown, Pennsylvania.

Sarah, my second daughter, obtained her Bachelor of Science Degree in Political Science and a Master of Science Degree in Constitutional Law from the University of Texas at Dallas. After this, she applied and got accepted to California Western School of Law. My wife and I knew law school

## Chapter 4 – Experiencing Spiritual Blessings in Christ

would be expensive and didn't know why she wanted to go to California where everything was expensive! She started schooling there and one day she posted her information and interests, including that she was a die-hard Dallas Cowboy's fan, on an online dating site. To her surprise, there was someone else who was also a die-hard Dallas Cowboy's fan who responded to her online posting. Their relationship progressed very quickly as they fell in love. When it came to the subject of who they should marry, I had told my girls the requirement I have for them was to marry a pastor's kid who had, at a minimum, a Master's Degree. I saw God's Grace and hand working in Sarah and David's lives.

To my surprise, Sarah called me up one day and said, "Dad, guess what, I am in love with a guy who is a pastor's kid and who has a Master's Degree in Divinity and he was a Senior Pastor at a church in Bellflower, California!" She also went on to say, "His name is David and he is white!" For the next two weeks, I could not rest and sleep! I was shocked. Why would she not marry someone from our own race? Then I reflected on my requirements that I placed on my girls regarding marriage. I had only two requests and it did not include a specific race for their life partner. God gave me peace about this after two weeks of unrest and Godly counsel from my family members. Anyway, Sarah's law school direction was quickly re-directed to line up with David's dream and vision, which was to serve inner-city children and families. Her law school lasted only for a semester, however, she found herself a life partner according to God's plan and purpose. God was working behind the scenes to bring Sarah and Rev. David Feiser together. They later relocated to Plano, Texas where David served as the student pastor for two years at Life Point Church. Again, the Lord, through a series of tough events and seasons, has

## Chapter 4 – Experiencing Spiritual Blessings in Christ

moved them from Plano, Texas to Washington, D.C. where Sarah is serving as a Recruiter for Global Mission Support and Justice Operations for International Justice Mission (IJM). Both Sarah and David have an inner peace about this direction and season of their lives as they are totally relying on God for the next steps in their lives.

The next event I want to share with you is also amazing. It just shows that God's Grace continues from one generation to the next. In our case, God blessed us with the same type of blessings and favor to my daughter, Hannah. Earlier, I shared how I ended up going to Washington University in St. Louis and now I want to share how my daughter Hannah ended up in St. Louis, one generation later! She had thought that she would go to an in-state university. Her high school, Sunnyvale High School, had a college fair. She was not looking for any booths besides Texas universities. While she was walking with her best friends, an underclassman came up to them and asked if they had some gum. My daughter, Hannah, jokingly said, "No, but you should go ask her," as she pointed to a random lady at a booth nearby. He went and asked her for gum. She opened a brand-new gum packet, and by this time, Hannah and her friends also went to her for gum. The trade-off was that they had to listen to what she had to say about Webster University. My daughter was waiting for the gum packet, but during this time she engaged in a conversation, asking if they offered the major she was interested in. Then Hannah asked her about their study abroad programs. To Hannah's surprise, Webster University in St. Louis had everything she was looking for in those categories. Then, because she had nothing to lose, she asked for a free t-shirt. The recruiter agreed to send it. She told Hannah that she would waive any of the application fees if they applied. Hannah took her e-mail address but didn't

## Chapter 4 – Experiencing Spiritual Blessings in Christ

think anything of it. She was an amazing recruiter. She sent the shirt, waived the application fee, and a week or so before the Presidential Scholar Application was due, she emailed her to apply for this prestigious scholarship. The minimum ACT score requirement was 26. Hannah only had 25 for the ACT score. She had tried three times in the past to improve it and the highest she could score on it was 25. She didn't even think to apply for this reason. The recruiter informed her to still apply, even though her score did not meet their requirement. All of her teachers and references worked diligently so she could apply. Hannah received an e-mail a month or so later saying she was a finalist and was invited for an interview at Webster for the scholarship. I went with her and supported her as she had a full day of interviews. Out of 150+ finalists, Hannah was selected for the Presidential Scholarship, which is the highest scholarship given at Webster, a private university. God was working behind the scenes again and this time in full force and might! She accepted the scholarship, they accepted all her dual credit courses from high school, (two year's worth) and she ended up being a junior when she was a freshman. This allowed her to study abroad for a year and truly become a global citizen. It allowed her to find a way to get her Master's Degree within four years and have a scholarship pay for it. She was able to graduate with a BA in Management, an MA in Human Resources Development, a minor in Marketing Communications, as well as a Certificate of Leadership. All her credentials got her an internship at Amazon during her first semester of her last year in school, which led to a full-time job offer. While everyone was stressing about what they would do after college, she had figured it out well before anyone else. That job took her to her dream city, Seattle. Since then, she has taken a year off to work in the mission field of Mumbai, India. She is helping the International

## Chapter 4 – Experiencing Spiritual Blessings in Christ

Justice Mission (IJM) with their mission of curbing and stopping human sex trafficking completely.

I have now been in the United States for over 43 years. God has blessed me immensely! In my life, three generations have seen and experienced the grace, goodness, and blessings of God! My wife and I are now grandparents, so the fourth generation has entered the scene! I am not worried or concerned about the future generations. He is faithful! His Grace is sufficient! I can say as the Apostle Paul did in Philippians 1:6, "Being confident of this, that He who began a good work in you will carry it on to completion until the day of Christ Jesus." He worked and continues to work behind the scenes by going before us like a good shepherd, preparing the way and making our surroundings safe, and comforting us even when we go through problems, so we can lie down and rest.

I am reminded of the "Post-Turtle" picture that I recently saw on the internet. It has a turtle on top of a fence post. The world will conclude the following three things: 1) the turtle did not get up there by itself 2) The turtle does not belong up there and 3) The turtle does not know what to do while he's up there. Someone had to place the turtle on top of the post. The turtle cannot, by itself, climb up to the top of the post. That's the way it has been in my life. The grace, goodness, and faithfulness of God has placed my family and me on top of many life posts! I call them God-ordained grace posts. When He places us there, He equips us with all the proper tools necessary to stay up there for a season of our life. He places us at the right place at the right time for the right purpose. And whenever someone asks me about a post my family and I are sitting upon, I will say, "It's all God's Grace and God placed us there on top of the post!"

## Chapter 4 – Experiencing Spiritual Blessings in Christ

I know God can take you and your life and position you on top of the post, just like the turtle. As God goes ahead of you, my prayer is that He will be placing you on these God-ordained posts of life, so you can also say with me, "God is a good God who is working behind the scenes for my good!"

I continue to experience God's Grace and favor in my life. I am learning and understanding the richness of this marvelous Grace that was so freely given to us in and through Christ our Savior and Lord! My prayer is that you will understand this marvelous Grace and that this book has helped you to gain a better understanding of this Grace that is so high, wide, rich and free! Come embrace and walk in this Grace with me!

Chapter 5 – What I Learned About Grace from My Pet Chickens

# CHAPTER 5

# What I Learned About Grace from My Pet Chickens

One day I got a call from Dixon, one of my friends from McAllen, Texas. He informed me about five chickens and a coop that I could have for free. The reason for this generous offer was the fact that the five chickens were in Joshi's backyard, Dixon's best friend in Carrollton, Texas. The neighbors had complained to the city officials about the chickens being loud and that they could not sleep. I heard from Joshi that if one chicken would lay an egg, the other four, (along with the one that laid the egg), would become a choir. The chickens had to go within a week. Joshi, in desperation, called Dixon in McAllen and told him about his situation. As this story was unfolding in real life, I started to understand more about the Grace of God. Buckle up, this story gets interesting.

The amazing thing about this whole situation is that my wife and I had wanted to raise chickens for a long time. We live in a home in a small town with three acres of land. In fact, I had investigated raising chickens a couple of years ago and looked up various designs of chicken coops, including the one on wheels. The whole set-up with chickens, feed, the feeder, and including a 10 x 10 chicken coop would cost about $1,000.00 to $1,500.00. So, we put the idea of raising chickens aside and just prayed about it and waited for His timing.

## Chapter 5 – What I Learned About Grace from My Pet Chickens

For the last several years my wife and I have been studying about rest, resting in the Lord for every situation and decision, and leaving it up to Him to bring things to pass. As a result, we started experiencing amazing victories in our lives when we gave things over to the Lord and waited upon Him for His best timing for our needs. We have been healed supernaturally, given creative ideas for our business, and made wiser decisions because of resting in Him. The amazing thing about the lifestyle of rest is that there is no worry or anxiety, but just an overall peace that you experience. When we received the call from Dixon, I felt peace about it personally. Then when I asked my wife about it, she also was excited and agreed with me and I knew it was God's timing for us to start raising chickens. The best part was that we got the chickens, the coop, and all of the feeding equipment free!

We said OK to Dixon and he gave me the contact information for Joshi. Joshi informed me that I needed to be there the upcoming weekend to help him out. You see, there was another friend of Joshi's that said he would come and get the chickens. But this friend was not interested in raising the chickens, but to kill them and make chicken curry out of them! Time was of the essence! Therefore, I loaded up some tools into my work truck and went there that weekend. It was at this point that I realized that I was really involved in saving the chickens from getting killed.

This newfound information put a whole new perspective into this whole situation. I was involved in a rescue mission of the chickens. Wasn't this the case with our Lord and Savior Jesus Christ, that over 2,000 years ago, He came from heaven and rescued us humans from the life of sin and death? He gave us new life in Him and set us up for eternal

## Chapter 5 – What I Learned About Grace from My Pet Chickens

life. We did not have to do anything but to be in His presence and accept His love for us. The five chickens had no clue that their life was in jeopardy and that if someone did not come in time to rescue them, they were going to be killed by someone with another motive. They were just going on their merry way and eating and drinking as usual. This is the way the devil wants us to go on with our lives, oblivious to the danger of sin and our need for God. But the Word of God tells us that the devil comes to steal, kill and destroy. The good news is that Jesus came to give life more abundantly. (John 10:10)

It was cold and windy that day and Joshi, his son, and I had to figure out a way to transfer the chickens safely to my backyard. It took about three hours in total to dismantle the chicken coop, load it up onto my truck, and safely put the chickens in cardboard boxes inside my truck. I could see Joshi's wife peeking through the window to see the rescue taking place. Later, I found out from Joshi that she was very happy to see the chickens go to a safe home where they would be well taken care of.

Joshi came in his car and helped me set up the chicken coop in my backyard. We also put a 10x10 chain fence around the chicken coop for their protection. Joshi left that day all rejoicing and happy, even though he had to give up the chickens and the coop. He was very happy that the chickens were saved from death. The Lord also brought to my mind about redemption. **Redemption** by definition, is an act of redeeming or atoning for a fault or mistake, or the state of being redeemed. In the chicken's case, the chickens were not at fault; someone else put them in a situation where their lives were put in jeopardy. Joshi had decided to have chickens in their backyard, not really knowing the

## Chapter 5 – What I Learned About Grace from My Pet Chickens

consequences for it. Adam and Eve made decisions in the Garden of Eden to eat from the tree of the knowledge of Good and Evil and sinned. Thus, all of humanity's life was put in jeopardy. Even though we didn't commit the sin back then with Adam, we all are thus born into sin. The consequences of sin are death. We were all destined to die as sinners, however, through the Grace of God, Jesus stepped into the picture and rescued us by giving His own life to satisfy the judgment of God. Thus, by the shed blood of Jesus Christ, we have been redeemed. In the case of the chickens, I did not have to die to save them, but you get the picture of how the rescue took place.

After we set up the chicken coop and fence, I went by that evening to the coop to see how they were doing. To my surprise, there was one egg that was laid that evening. I guess you can say that one of the chickens showed us appreciation by blessing us with an egg the very first day. Now the chickens are living a much better life. Initially, I was very protective of the chickens. I would keep them inside the 10-foot x 10-foot fenced area. My wife would tell me constantly to let them out so they can enjoy their freedom. I am glad she got me out of that mindset. She was right! Now during the day, they are let out of the chicken coop to roam around the three acres of land to experience all the bountiful blessings. Every morning, they are lined up near the door of the coop and can't wait to get out to experience the land filled with milk and honey. This was a land that they never expected to be blessed with. We recently tilled a large garden area where we are planning to plant vegetables. As soon as the chickens are released from the coop, they do a beeline to the newly tilled garden. They know that there is plenty of food there for them to eat and partake of. They are no longer in a small backyard inside a coop, but instead, they are

## Chapter 5 – What I Learned About Grace from My Pet Chickens

enjoying the good life of security and plenty. The chickens have found a new life of enjoyment and plenty. Because of this, we are on average rewarded with three to four eggs per day. This validates to me that they are very grateful to us! We went after the chickens, we rescued them, we provided for them, we set everything up for them, we put a fence around them for protection, we make sure their coop is safe in the night, we planned to provide them with food and water and continue to do so daily, we blessed them!

This is exactly what our Lord Jesus Christ did for us. He chose us and came after us and rescued us from a life of sin, bondage, uncertainty, doubts, and fear to an uncommon life of bountiful blessings. He continues to bless us materially, emotionally, spiritually, and physically. God had already planned this life out for us from the beginning. It is exciting to know that our God is such a loving God who rescues us and gives us freedom! I am reminded of the God of Glory (goodness) represented in Ephesians chapter 1. He takes us to high places of blessing in Him. He had us in mind even before the foundation of the world. We were the focus of His love. He took lots of pleasure in planning this out for us. He gave us Jesus, His beloved son, as a gift to us and the world. We are free from the penalties and punishment for our sins because of what Jesus did on the cross for us and we are justified because of His resurrection (Romans 4:25). He has abundantly made us free. He planned everything out and provided everything for us. We have abundant life in Christ, and in Him, all our hopes and dreams are fulfilled. All this is guaranteed and sealed by the Holy Spirit and that is amazing.

I am just thankful that God brought these chickens in my life to show me the richness of God's grace! Even before the foundation of the world, He had us in His mind to rescue us and set us free. He wanted to bless us with every spiritual blessing. He wanted us to experience heaven on earth. I want to pray the same prayer that Paul prayed now for you:

> *"I ask—ask the God of our Master, Jesus Christ, the God of glory—to make you intelligent and discerning in knowing him personally, your eyes focused and clear, so that you can see exactly what it is he is calling you to do, grasp the immensity of this glorious way of life he has for his followers, oh, the utter extravagance of his work in us who trust him—endless energy, boundless strength!"*

As the owners of these chickens, my wife and I are gaining knowledge through experience and research. Research shows that there are up to 30 different sounds chickens make. We are finding out that chickens are very vocal and conversational critters. Hopefully, as we pay attention to them, we will be able to learn to understand and speak their language, too. It's been now about two months with these chickens and I have learned a lot about God's grace and goodness. They are finding out that if they come in our presence, they don't have to be fearful, but loved and protected. It is all about the goodness of a heavenly father that provides and protects His children. My wife and I have been able to provide and protect the chickens. I am constantly thinking ahead of how I can make their lives better! This is the way we should see our Heavenly Father. He is always good and full of Grace and we are His beloved sons and daughters!

Every day, when we see the chickens happy, it makes us happy. Our Lord is the same way! I pray that this book has been a blessing to you. I thank you for taking the time to understand this wonderful grace that is so rich and free! It is not based on our performance in any way. It is fully based on Jesus' death on the cross of Calvary. Every sin, judgment, punishment, guilt, shame, curse, sickness, condemnation, has been dealt with on the cross of Calvary! Walk in the new and rich understanding of God's Grace and you will enjoy life to the fullest! Ephesians 3:20 says that:

> *God can do anything, you know—far more than you could ever imagine or guess or request in your wildest dreams! He does it not by pushing us around but by working within us, his Spirit deeply and gently within us. (MSG)*

Let the Holy Spirit of God work in us and then let us work out what He worked in us! Let me leave you with this priestly blessing from Numbers 6:24-26:

> *"The Lord Bless You, and Keep You;*
> *The Lord Make His Face to Shine Upon You,*
> *And be gracious to you;*
> *The Lord lift His Countenance on You,*
> *And give you Peace."*

## Chapter 5 – What I Learned About Grace from My Pet Chickens

The Grace I Never Knew

The Grace I Never Knew

## ABOUT THE AUTHOR

Mathew's passion is to remind his audience about God's Kingdom, and that we are all part of a Kingdom and Culture where God is a good God and God is madly in love with its citizens. God's agape love gave us a King, Jesus Christ who is the head of this Kingdom. Their teaching reminds the believers of their identity in Christ and empowers them to live their lives to the fullest God-given potential.

Pastor Mathew is a graduate of the Church of God Ministerial Internship Program. Mathew is also an Ordained Minister with the Assemblies of God. Mathew is a Counselor certified by the American Association of Christian Counselors. He is also a licensed Professional Engineer with the State of Texas and holds a Master of Science Degree in Mechanical Engineering from Washington University in St. Louis and a Master of Business Administration. He is the President & CEO of RSH Engineering, Inc.

He is married to Sweet Soffee and blessed with four children, Remarkable Rebekah, Smart Sarah, Happy Hannah, and Sharp Samuel, and two super son-in-law's, Ben and David and two God-given grandchildren, Joseph and Luke.

You can reach Mathew at:
Rev. Mathew Joseph
(972)523-5746
president@rshengineering.com
www.rshengineering.com

The Grace I Never Knew

The Grace I Never Knew

The Grace I Never Knew

The Grace I Never Knew

## Disclaimer & Copyright Information

Some of the events, locales, and conversations have been recreated from memories. In order to maintain their anonymity, in some instances, the names of individuals and places have been changed. As such, some identifying characteristics and details may have changed.

Although the author and publishers have made every effort to ensure that the information in this book was correct at press time, the authors and publishers do not assume and hereby disclaim any liability to any party for any loss, damage, or disruption caused by errors or omissions, whether such errors or omissions result from negligence, accident, or any other cause. The author is solely responsible for the content of this story.

All quotes, unless otherwise noted,
are attributed to the Author or to the Holy Bible.

Cover illustration, book design, and production
Copyright © 2018 by Tribute Publishing LLC
www.TributePublishing.com

Scripture references are copyrighted by www.BibleGateway.com
which is operated by the Zondervan Corporation, L.L.C

# The Grace I Never Knew

The Grace I Never Knew

## NOTES

## NOTES

## NOTES

## NOTES

## NOTES

The Grace I Never Knew

www.ingramcontent.com/pod-product-compliance
Lightning Source LLC
Chambersburg PA
CBHW020428010526
44118CB00010B/475